LET'S
GET
IT!

LET'S GET IT!

HUSTLE AND GRIND YOUR WAY TO PERSONAL EMPOWERMENT

ADARSH VIJAY MUDGIL, M.D.

Selected for New York "Super Doctor" Listings & Castle Connolly Top Doctor

WITH MICHAEL J. COFFINO

Foreword by NFL Hall of Famer Marshall Faulk

ISBN: 978-1-78324-182-8

Book design by Wordzworth
www.wordzworth.com

To the two strongest women I know:
my mother and my wife,
whose unfailing grit inspires me daily.

CONTENTS

ACKNOWLEDGMENTS

Nearly three years ago when I decided it was time for me to do more, touch more lives with positivity, and give back on a larger scale, Michael Litman, an entrepreneur I admire, helped me crystallize my ambition. Over a casual dinner, Mike recommended five books that I devoured in a matter of weeks: *The E-Myth Revisited*, *The One Thing*, *The 10X Rule*, *The 4-Hour Workweek*, and *Crushing It*. I never stopped reading, and the rest is history, as they say. Thanks, Mike.

I couldn't have written this book without Michael Coffino, my cowriter. I'm a big believer in going with your gut, and boy am I glad I did. Of the hundreds of résumés I received, Michael was the first (and only) writer I interviewed. I felt an instant connection. Maybe it's a New York thing—who knows? In any event, I loved the process of writing this book, particularly the therapeutic early stages when we spent hours capturing and dissecting my story.

I'm blessed to have had many mentors through the years, but a few deserve special mention. Thank you, Mr. McCarthy, my fifth-grade teacher, for believing in a bullied, bespectacled brown kid. Thank you to Dr. David Kriegel and Dr. Ed Heilman, who taught me how to doctor and mentor, but, more importantly, showed me that it's okay to "do me" in both roles.

Thank you to Sami Khan, my buddy from college, who ignited my hustle.

Thank you to Rahsaan Robinson, my personal trainer, who I consider one of my best friends. Much of this book was born out of the conversations we shared through the years while pumping iron.

Thank you to my social media community, whose messages and posts offer a steady stream of continual inspiration. Thank you to my podcast guests, who generously share themselves with me and my audience.

Thank you to the other members of "The Mudgil Five," my nuclear family. My wife, Vanita, keeps me in check, puts up with my antics, and loves me unconditionally. My beautiful children, Meera, Deven, and Jai have infinitely expanded the love in my heart.

Last, thank you to my mother, who defines the word selfless.

FOREWORD

I assumed we'd heard all we needed about self-motivation and empowerment—that when it came to personal growth and achievement, what it takes to succeed, and how we can become the masters of our lives, no more could be said, and no more needed to be said. I thought the market for personal inspiration material was oversaturated.

I got it wrong.

Dr. Adarsh Vijay Mudgil's *Let's Get It!*, like his powerful social media platform, is a game changer. It alters the landscape with its straight talk, core wisdom, constant optimism, and powerful simplicity.

Dr. Mudgil is not only a new voice with a fresh perspective, but the message he's so well packaged is also timely. It arrives at a moment of national and international stress, when we need more instructive reminders of our individual self-worth, the vastness of our personal potential, and how, with the right mindset, we can become the best person we can be.

As Dr. Mudgil candidly recognizes throughout this book, the path forward is not free of difficulty, stumbling blocks, and failure. On the contrary, all paths worth taking are chock-full of problems that challenge, test, and change us. Indeed, as *Let's Get It!* advocates, the speed bumps along the way are essential and worth welcoming. Bring them on.

At its deepest level, the book has this core truth: regardless of the nature and extent of the challenges we face, we each have the ability to realize contentment and ways to express our uniqueness, as long as we're honest with ourselves, make the commitment, dig our heels in, and get after it.

Everyone isn't dealt the same cards in life. We don't carry the same burdens. Fairness isn't always a reasonable expectation; far from it. Each of us comes packaged with our own set of troubles, flaws, and demons. We all have hurdles to overcome.

The beauty of *Let's Get It!* is how it lays out our common ground. Dr. Mudgil's straightforward approach to self-empowerment assumes nothing other than the simmering power we each have inside us that we can use to make it happen. It begins and ends by highlighting the importance of understanding who we are, what makes us special, and what action steps to take in order to make our dreams and aspirations more than wishful thinking, but realities that align with our essence.

Let's Get It! makes it clear that there's no formula for success, no quick fix for what we want out of life. It's all about what Dr. Mudgil aptly calls the "hustle and grind." Finding our inner strength, understanding our weaknesses and limitations, having a core set of values, and building from there is the key.

Let's Get It! has a no-nonsense, consciousness-raising quality that readers will find refreshing. The book challenges us to think about our lives both narrowly, in terms of charting our individual place in the world, and broadly—how we can impact others and our communities. It's all about exerting control over our own destinies.

As Dr. Mudgil puts it, "Time is a diminishing asset, and life is too precious to spend doing the bidding of others."

Let's get it!

Marshall Faulk

PREFACE

This book is the natural outgrowth of a personal redirection that I, quite frankly, did not see coming.

A few years ago, I had what many would call an aha moment—an insight that dramatically changed the course of the path I was on. By all accounts and traditional measures, I'd made it to a cherished destination. I'd achieved personal and professional success, the "bling" that comes with it, and accomplishments that drew heartfelt praise and widespread congratulations. I'd arrived.

And wasn't that what it was all about? Wasn't that the end game?

To put things into perspective, it all started with my mother's story. She's an Indian immigrant who escaped a dreadful marriage, leaving her a single parent in a new country with two young sons. One by one, she helped her own parents and siblings emigrate from India until there were nine of us living in a roach infested three-bedroom apartment in a Brooklyn housing development. Although some of my fondest memories are from my time in that apartment, looking back, it's hard to imagine how we all crammed into such a small space.

When my older brother was about to start high school, we moved to the south shore of Long Island to a solidly middle class, largely blue-collar neighborhood, to take advantage of public schooling opportunities. To say I stuck out like a sore thumb would be a dramatic understatement. First off, I was the only Indian kid in my grade, and one of maybe three or four in the entire school district. It was different than being in Brooklyn! The only other minority groups represented in a sea of white were a handful of Hispanic students and one or two Asians. There were no Black students. To top it off, I had donned glasses since kindergarten and my wardrobe largely consisted of my brother's seven-year-old hand me downs. I basically had a fluorescent target on my back begging to be bullied—and bullied I was!

Although we were comfortable in our new home on Long Island, we certainly didn't live a life that resembled that of my new friends. We almost never ate out, and in the rare instance we did (maybe once or twice a year), it was usually Pizza Hut, and only if we found a coupon in that week's PennySaver. I couldn't dare ask for brand clothing, designer sneakers, or cable television.

Lebron James shared a great line in his HBO show *The Shop* when describing the transition from his childhood neighborhood to an all-White Catholic high school, "Bread, cereal, chips, doughnuts, all that s–t is on top of the refrigerator. When I got to high school was the first time I knew about a pantry." That basically sums up the wonder I felt whenever visiting a friend's home who had cable television, name brand potato chips in their cupboard, or Haagen-Dazs ice cream in their freezer—clearly, they were rich!

Growing up education was paramount and extracurricular activities minimal. My mother provided whatever we needed for academics, but that was about it. I learned early on to be resourceful and enterprising to get things I wanted, an early version of the hustle and grind mindset discussed in this book. I did whatever I had to do to put some dollars in my pocket, paper routes, landscaping, shoveling snow, and pizza delivery.

One of my favorite jobs was valet parking cars on the posh north shore of Long Island, where fancy people with fancy cars lived in fancy homes. With the mansions, chic restaurants and country clubs, it was all a fantasy world to me. I couldn't fathom the wealth. How did people get to live in these homes, drive such cars, or belong to a country club? Who were these people? Heck, I couldn't imagine eating at any of the restaurants where I parked cars!

Fast forward twenty years. Overcoming humble beginnings, I built a thriving dermatology practice on Fifth Avenue in Manhattan and another on Long Island. I'd gained coveted professional standing and respect and boasted numerous accolades and honors. I had a gorgeous and loving wife who enjoyed her own professional success, and we had three beautiful, blossoming children. I owned a fancy home in the ritzy Long Island suburb just described, both my business offices, and a fleet of fancy cars. I played golf regularly. I had long-term financial security and freedom. I had, from what I could tell, it all.

But I began to feel that something wasn't right; that despite the glittery accoutrements, I really didn't have it all. I felt an unfamiliar emptiness inside.

Don't get me wrong. I wasn't ungrateful. On the contrary, I knew I was living a blessed life, particularly when compared to the challenges my family faced early in my life. I was proud of what I'd accomplished—it was what I'd set out to do—and what I'd overcome to get there. Whatever complaints I had along the way were few and minor in the larger scheme of things. My day-to-day world was more than good; it was great.

But for the first time, I felt incomplete, when everything around me said I should feel the opposite. Worse, I began to feel adrift—a little lost, and no longer as grounded as I'd been in years past. Initially it made no sense. It confused me. I'd followed my passion with an unyielding, intense focus to arrive exactly where I was: at the success I'd set my eyes on. I'd followed the professional playbook pretty much the way it was designed, and, a few expected hiccups notwithstanding, I'd come out on top.

So what was the problem? Why wasn't I feeling fulfilled?

I retraced my steps and took a deep look within to gain an understanding of what success meant to me. I became self-critical, examining my values as they played out in real time and not from a philosophical perch. Upon reflection, my journey seemed well played, but now I was coasting—making do on autopilot. Even though I continued to put in the time and effort at work and my professional success stayed constant, I was in a rut. My life had become too easy, and that, ironically, made me uneasy. I'd lost my grind; my edge. The passion was gone, my creativity muted. I was stagnant. I was starring in my own personal version of *Groundhog Day*.

I began to see that success, which I knew could be defined in a wide range of ways, is more process than object, and that the journey we take to express ourselves and achieve what's important to us is never-ending, of utmost importance, and subject to constant retooling and redirection. The risk is landing on a plateau and staying put—resting on one's laurels, as it were.

I began to see the path to success as a constant flow of transformation and broadening that endlessly yields new ways to become fulfilled.

This meant embracing a few interrelated questions. Where do I go next? What am I capable of doing now? And, perhaps the pièce de résistance, what do I want my personal legacy to be?

Up until then I'd been, appropriately, focused on finding myself, building a career, and having a family. The time had come for me to expand my impact, reach out beyond the life I'd built, and influence and connect with others in positive and lasting ways. I could see that, through the years, I'd laid a strong foundation that enabled me to help others chart their own paths to success. Why not attempt to touch as many people as possible in precisely this way?

I wanted others to know a simple truth: if I could accomplish what I did, they could accomplish what they wanted too.

My passion returned, and a new vision revealed itself to me. I looked to social media as an outlet that could help me spread this message of positivity and self-empowerment. In February 2018, I committed to posting on Instagram once a day. I haven't missed a day since. I'm blessed to have a significant following, which continues to grow. The subjects of my posts generally fall into two categories, the first being dermatology and the second being mindset, motivation, and self-empowerment. I truly delight in sharing my insights with a wide audience.

I've especially enjoyed the question-and-answer posts—these give me the opportunity to help an individual find or clarify their path, identify challenges, and tackle hurdles in a constructive way. These interactions inspire me more than I could have ever imagined and continue to give me lasting satisfaction.

I also launched *The Dr. Mudgil Podcast*, where I interview people who have achieved success in their own ways and have valuable advice and insights to share. I love the personal nature of these sessions and how they allow listeners (and me!) to find themselves in the content. The podcasts—more than thirty at the time of publication—consistently inspire me.

This book became the natural next step. I wanted a medium that could distill everything I was trying to say into a single format. It hasn't been easy—it's required commitment and drive or, as I like to say, hustle and grind.

The process has been therapeutic, giving me greater personal insight. It's also helped clarify and refine the message I've been trying to get out into the world. The fluid movement of constant learning and change I've come to embrace has allowed me to help others find and manage their own paths to success.

I hope that what follows helps you source your internal power in order to reach your goals—whatever they are—and achieve whatever success means to you. Let's get it!

INTRODUCTION

"Wise is the one who learns to dumb it down."
-CURTIS TYRONE JONES

Writing this book underscored a simple truth about achieving success on our own terms: the definition is individual. There is no formula. There is no hack.

When all is said and done, it boils down to a firm mindset about how to exert control over each of the pieces that make up our lives, and what we need to do day after day to progress toward the goals we crave.

To be sure, there are many details and nuances involved in making it happen—many component parts, as discussed throughout the book. But each derives from the same place: a willingness to take charge of the process that will make our aspirations real.

Do we let life simply happen to us or do we actively shape our destinies by hustling and grinding toward the goals we set?

At the most basic level, it begins with honest self-examination. We can't put an effective game plan for success into motion without first taking an in-depth look at who we are, what makes us tick, what holds us back, what our basic strengths are, and what changes we need to make to get to where we want to land.

Everything we do reflects who we are. We need to understand who that person is before we can accomplish much of anything. Otherwise, we cede control to other forces, and when we do, we leave opportunity on the table. Being aware and honest about who we are is the first step toward genuinely believing in ourselves and becoming self-empowered.

The foundation—what gives life to it all—is our value system. It may be that we have incorporated values into our lives without much, or any, thought, and that some of these values may not serve us well. But wherever our initial values come from, they're reflected in everything we say, the decisions we make, and the actions we take. Part of knowing ourselves, and what's integral to taking control of our lives, is having a core set of values that we consciously select as our guideposts for everything we do and how we shape the destiny we deserve.

Sometimes control means yielding, or having an abiding willingness to tap into the wisdom of others and let those who came before us give us a boost. As I discuss later, success leaves clues: the accomplishments and track records of those we admire can be a treasure trove of helpful hints, information, techniques, and ideas about how to get things done. While ingenuity is always an option (we don't ever want to ignore the freshness of our ideas), looking to successful people—especially mentors and role models—and following in their footsteps gives us focus and demonstrates a willingness to shun pride in favor of learning and bettering ourselves.

The same is true for connecting with others in our everyday lives, whether they're family, friends, coworkers and professional colleagues, or, yes, strangers. The connective part of our individual worlds, along with how we engage fellow human beings and the empathy and affirmation we impart to them, are essential to becoming whole. We can't live in isolation without impairing our ability to become our best selves. How we connect with others puts our imprint on the world.

Still, no matter how much we learn from others or how well we engage with the humanity of the people we meet, we won't have control over the direction of our lives unless we honor criticism and capitalize on the inherent value of failure. If we turn a deaf ear toward criticism and retreat into the dark shadows of failure, we merely empower the forces that limit and stymie us. The choice is straightforward: either embrace criticism and failure and convert them into something powerful, or allow them to shut us down and keep us stagnant.

This applies with equal force to the choices we make about how we treat our bodies, both inside and out. This can be a complex challenge, as I explore later on in this book. The path to ultimate contentment will leave us wanting, however, unless we take care of our bodies in a thoughtful and vigilant way, which includes both physical conditioning and overall health and wellness. It may be self-evident, but sound nutritional habits and a rigorous exercise regime are critical to achieving success and exerting control over our lives.

In the end, the path to self-empowerment is something we each have to determine for ourselves. The journey that follows reflects what worked for me—it's no more or less than one person's application of the mindset this book explores. We can each achieve success in our own way and express the best of who we are.

I hope you'll see parts of yourself in this book and find ways to redraw or enhance your road map to personal contentment. Let's get it.

1

Find Your Gift, Mind the Process

"Changing your mindset is a game changer."
—FRANK SONNENBERG

Everyone ends up where they belong.

This isn't meant as a harsh, elitist, or socially insensitive comment. Nor do I mean to say we have no choice in our fates. It is, rather, to convey that our respective destinies are drawn from the paths we carve out for ourselves, whether we do so by using decisive focus, mechanically plodding along, or passively riding the wave of life.

It all comes down to the mindset we apply to the processes we undertake in our lives, knowing our strengths and limitations, and adapting accordingly.

Sometimes we get help along the way—events or people that jolt us into seeing the light and gaining deeper insight into ourselves. We can all use an occasional nudge—or push—into good sense and reality. I had three such experiences that helped me reconfigure my mindset, provided me with more clarity into what makes me tick, and ultimately set me on a more productive path—one with intense purpose.

Two occurred relatively early in my life.

Before my brother and I began any serious thinking about what we wanted to be when we grew up, our mother, a medical doctor and single parent, made it clear she expected us both to pursue medical careers. The reasons for this were many, the most important of which being the stability that her career in medicine provided—it had enabled her to escape the confines of an abusive marriage and raise her two boys on her own.

My mother became a doctor against enormous odds, displaying a single-mindedness that was deeply inspirational. Although I never knew my father, I understand he was a frightful and abusive man. He was a psychiatrist and a raging schizophrenic who, rather than seek professional help for his mental illness, self-medicated. His psychotic episodes were suffocating, and they wreaked havoc in our family. Further, he forbade my mother—who, like himself, had gone to medical school in India—from taking the United States Medical Licensing Examination (USMLE), even though my family lived in New York City at the time. He feared, appropriately, that if she passed the exam, she would leave him, as passing would enable her to pursue her own career in the U.S. and gain her independence. Undaunted by my father's oppressive oversight, my mother was determined to obtain her U.S. medical license to create a better life for herself, my brother, and me—so much so that she rode the New York City subway through the night with no destination, studying for her licensing exam in secret. Passing was her ticket out of a dreadful domestic situation.

She is my hero, and I draw strength every day from her brave struggle and conquest.

During our childhood years, my mother had a mantra she'd repeatedly say to my brother and me: "You both need to be able to stand on your own two feet." Her humble career as a government doctor enabled her to do just that as a single parent raising two boys. In her mind, the stability of a career in medicine was the path to independence for both of us. Moreover, she viewed a career in medicine as honorable, noble, and morally upstanding.

My brother and I never seriously challenged the path she chose for us. If you were to ask any of my childhood friends what they thought I was going to be when I grew up, going back to when I was five or six years old, the answer was always "a doctor." My brother, who was a stronger student than I, desperately wanted to attend one of the Ivy League colleges that admitted him. But my mother, fearing he would stray from the medical career path, essentially forced him to attend a seven-year medical program straight out of high school. This was perhaps a less prestigious route than obtaining an Ivy League degree, but to her way of thinking, it was a foolproof way to ensure he became a doctor, which was the ultimate and essential goal.

My mother swiftly and firmly shut down any slight pushback we gave. When my brother was an undergraduate, he expressed a desire for a different direction. "I want to go to law school," he said. Fair enough, I thought. But not missing a beat, my mother replied, "That's fine, not a problem at all, as long as you go to medical school first." Case closed; we both became doctors. (And if you're wondering, my brother never went to law school after getting his medical degree.)

It took me awhile to see the lessons in what my mom did. There was no question that she strong armed us. She had the power. She was the sole voice of authority in the family. And, as a parent who'd climbed more than her share of mountains, she knew something we didn't about long-term stability and success. But it was more than that. She knew our DNA. She knew our natural gifts, and where we were apt to blossom. She was dictating our path, yes, but she was also teaching us to build on who we were for the rest of our lives. As I grew older, I could appreciate her foresight. It helped me know who I was, who I could be, and how I could grow into myself.

When we're young, it's natural—if not inevitable—to follow the lead of the adults in our lives, to emulate how they do things. In our early lives, we have little else to go on. At some point, however, it's essential to focus on how *we* best do things within the parameters of who we are and what makes us unique. We must become wary of the tendency to idealize a model of who we think we are, or self-limitations about who we think we're unlikely to be, and instead be mindful that others' methods, inclinations, and gifts are theirs and not ours. We have to learn to embrace our unique qualities, characteristics, wants and desires, and the processes that serve us well.

Our natural gifts may not be the ones we thought we had when we were young and naturally disposed to emulate those we held in high regard. Only honest self-examination will free us to discover and appreciate the fullness of what our gifts truly are.

Once we know our innate gifts, the challenge becomes figuring out how best to leverage and build on them. Standing alone, they're not enough. We all have tendencies to get comfortable with what comes easily for us and use it as a crutch or an excuse to not push the envelope. When this happens, we're apt to avoid the kind of effort needed to expand our reach and improve our performance.

I learned this lesson the hard way in high school.

During my sophomore year, I was slated to provide a speech at a Model United Nations competition at Duke University. I was the representative for a relatively unknown African country, and I had to expound on some weighty topic. As I'd done with most things academic at that point of my life, I thought I could wing it with minimal preparation. I had the gift of gab; I could hold my own in any setting simply by standing up in front of listeners and letting loose. Blinded by my perceived swagger, I thought, I've got this. I'm good at speaking.

But I'd never performed in front of hundreds of people before, much less on a stage, alone. In my naivete, I didn't appreciate how far public speaking at that level was from waxing about this and that in front of friends and family. I could banter with the best of them and I was an aficionado of bullshitting, but I had no clue about the dynamics and art of public speaking.

I stepped to the podium and scanned the assembled multitudes. I fixated on what seemed like an abyss of countless faces eagerly waiting to hear pearls of wisdom spill from my lips. My heart started racing. I felt off balance. I lost sight of what I wanted to say and why I was up there in the first place. I could only think about the peering eyes of the crowd, and I literally froze. I was unable to utter a word, and I began to sweat. I became overwhelmed with embarrassment and couldn't shake the paralyzing feelings of panic. I was on an island with no hope of rescue.

I didn't give the speech—I mumbled some stupidity and gave up the stage. Talk about humbling. I'd suffered, I would later realize, a full-fledged panic attack, one of two I would experience in my life.

I knew I'd messed up badly. I'd captained a disaster. I hadn't prepared for something I was ill-equipped to handle without advanced planning. I'd deluded myself. It taught me that my social gift of repartee didn't translate into the gift of public speaking.

But I knew something else, too. I knew I would never put myself in a situation like that again. I knew I could take steps to do better, to be better. If I ever wanted to address an assembled group in a formal or semi-formal way, I had to take steps to get strong and comfortable in that setting. I didn't have a natural gift for public speaking, if there even was one.

I took that specific lesson to heart and got to know myself better. Whenever opportunities arose, even to this day, I would prepare with fierce and focused diligence, whether speaking at weddings and conferences or, more recently, on television shows. I did what I needed to do to get comfortable in front of a crowd. I embraced my limitations and worked tirelessly on improving myself.

But the power of this lesson was more fundamental than I realized at the time. Despite my awful experience at the Model United Nations, I didn't extend what I learned from that incident to other aspects of my life. Sometimes it takes more than one embarrassing experience to get wise on a broader scale. As they say, old habits die hard. I'd learned my lesson about public speaking, but I still didn't fully appreciate the underlying principle of facing my limitations and adjusting accordingly. It took a brutally candid comment from a college friend to pry my eyes open and teach me the fullness of the lesson.

Before getting into the details of what would turn out to be the most trajectory-altering conversation of my life, let me provide some background and context. Despite doing well toward the end of high school, I floundered during my freshman year, thus crushing my chances of attending an Ivy League university. Not surprisingly, each one rejected me, as did other elite colleges on the *U.S. News & World Report*'s "top 25" list. I ended up at Emory University in Atlanta, my safety school, which I'd never visited. I accepted their admission offer sight unseen and showed up on the first day of school with no idea what to expect.

If there is any testament to the strength of the Long Island public school system, it was my performance at Emory. I barely attended any classes, had the time of my life, and graduated with a 3.97 GPA. The funny thing is, my mom threatened to pull me out of Emory and send me to state school after I earned a 3.76 GPA my first college semester. She was disinclined to pay Emory's hefty private-school tuition if I wasn't bringing home perfect scores! She was serious, and I knew it. Needless to say, I had nothing but 4.0 grade averages thereafter.

The truth is, my academic performance at Emory gives me little pride. I did the absolute minimum required to get an A in each class. My approach had nothing to do with learning—it was a game to me. I set out to determine what it took to get that A and the rest fell into place, allowing me to coast.

I brought the same mindset to medical school at Stony Brook University, on Long Island. I got good grades, but I wasn't about to get any awards or distinguish myself. I was solidly positioned in the middle of my class of one hundred students and, at the time, that satisfied me. After all, medical school talent was abundant. Most of my classmates hailed from the Ivy League schools that rejected me. I honestly thought I was doing my best, and I was content being a touch above average in a sea of rich academic talent.

The searing reality was that I was getting by because I possessed a wicked memory. My memory wasn't something I'd earned; it was a natural gift, and it allowed me to manage academics with relative ease. I could, for example, read textbook material in fifteen minutes that took most students an hour or two to read, and I could call up the content verbatim, as if emblazoned on my eyes. I may not have understood everything I read, or even learned much, but I could regurgitate what I read like an audio textbook. Drawing on my natural aptitude for memorization, I could, without doing much more, manage school well enough. I was replicating what I'd done in my undergraduate coursework, which deluded me into thinking that I had a winning formula. Why not do the same thing in medical school? Memorize material, take the tests, and move on. I could skip class as well, using transcribed class notes to memorize what I needed to cough up at exam time.

But I was kidding myself. I wasn't learning much. I wasn't building a rich foundation for practicing medicine. I was, for all intents and purposes, skating—gaming the system in my own way. I was mindlessly results-oriented. I was willfully ignoring the process of learning.

Then my good friend Sami Khan, from my Emory days, called me on it. Sami was a stellar, 4.0-average student throughout our time as undergraduates. His approach to academics was more about learning; it was pure. Although he stayed at Emory to attend medical school, Sami visited me in Long Island the summer after our first years. We compared notes. He'd continued with his high level of performance, hovering at the top of his class. When I shared where I stood, buried in the middle of my class and expending little effort, he responded, without a hint of humor, "For once in your life, why don't you just try."

Wow!

That one sentence, delivered with a blend of candor, frustration, and genuine concern, hit me right between the eyes. Sami knew me. In fact, in this respect at least, he knew me better than I knew myself. He knew I was wasting my gifts; that I was taking shortcuts and jeopardizing my success and my ability to realize my potential. While I was taken aback at first, I quickly saw that Sami had given me a profound gift.

His comment inspired me to look more closely at the interplay between natural gifts and limitations on the one hand, and success on the other. I could see that natural gifts guaranteed nothing. Superathletes like Michael Jordan and the late Kobe Bryant had enormous natural gifts as athletes, but the lion's share of their success came from how they used those gifts, and how much time and effort they devoted to building on them. They didn't rest on their laurels and take the easy way out; they leveraged their gifts into something much greater. They doubled down on their talents, and by doing so, they became *the* elite among a sea of other elite athletes.

While few have the natural gifts of a Michael Jordan or a Kobe Bryant, we all have our own natural strengths. Over time, if we pay attention to ourselves, understand what makes us more productive, exploit strengths, and overcome weaknesses, we can make decisions and choices and engineer a life process with the right mindset.

Stated differently, we can mind the process.

Thanks to Sami, changing my mindset from studying to pass exams to studying to learn was a game changer.

Using my God-given talent (my exceptional memory), I began for the first time to learn how to learn. My second year of medical school was the first time I understood how to truly study, and boy, did it open my eyes. It was like I'd discovered a precious secret.

The crazy thing is, I wasn't working any harder. I still rarely went to class and maintained a robust social life. The difference was that I was working smarter and with purpose. I was studying to learn, and by doing so, I became able to interconnect the complex processes of the body's various organ systems to pathology and pharmacology with an ease that others struggled with. It made medical school easier and a hell of a lot more fun!

Viewing our lives from a safe and uncluttered distance—as if sitting high on a perch above ourselves with a bird's-eye view of what we're feeling, saying, and doing—is probably the most telling perspective we can have. This vantage point, when we can manage it, yields a meaningful read on what's happening to us in the moment. Distance brings the kind of clarity that teaches us who we are and where we're headed. Moreover, it allows us to distill our actions and personal processes down to their essence and evaluate what's most effective for us.

Never stop asking these questions. How do I work best? What's the most effective way to tailor methods to my natural skills and shortcomings?

I have an approach I favor whenever I'm evaluating the quality of this process. It employs two broad categories: "bad busy" and "good busy."

I divide bad busy into two groups. The first—and the most unredeeming of the two—occurs when we spend unproductive time with poor or no intent. We're going through the motions, spinning our wheels, and wasting valuable time. Here's an example from a seemingly mundane routine that I think speaks volumes.

Years ago, I had an employee who took an hour or more each day to order her lunch. On her computer screen, she would have eight different Seamless or Grubhub menus open, and she'd go back and forth, fretting as she cross-referenced the menus, trying to figure out what she wanted for lunch that day, deciding and undeciding in a predictable pattern. It was an ingrained ritual from which she never wavered. While she toiled and anguished over what to order, work didn't get done. She was trading productive time for unproductive time, failing to take advantage of peak times in the day. It was maddening, and an example of bad busy with no intent.

She embraced her indecisiveness as an unavoidable personal trait rather than self-evaluating and finding her way off the treadmill of inefficiency. Knowing that this was an unproductive daily ritual, she could've minimized the impact of her indecisiveness, for example, by making her lunch decisions the night before or prior to when work began in earnest each day.

The takeaway here is the importance of recognizing a limiting trait and figuring out a way to minimize its impact. I've shared this observation with medical students I counsel. They all study hard, spending countless hours packing an enormous amount of information into their heads. But just like I did before Sami set me straight, so many of them approach studying as the destination—a requisite hurdle standing in their way of a medical degree. Like I first did in medical school, they often don't appreciate the importance of *learning* the material in contrast to memorizing it to pass an exam. By engaging in mindless short-term cramming, they were missing out on the learning process—a cogent example of bad busy with poor intent.

Then we have bad busy with good intent, where we're trying to do the right thing, but for whatever reason aren't getting it done. Our eyes are on the prize and we have the motivation and the work ethic, but our methods aren't up to snuff because they're not designed carefully to achieve the goals we seek.

Here's a personal example that illustrates the concept. When I first started playing golf ten years ago, I was determined to get better. I knew that practice, and a lot of it, was essential. I went to the driving range and pounded away at hundreds of balls for hours on end—day in, day out. I wasn't a natural at golf; I didn't have the gift, so I focused on improving how I played the game. I had good intentions, the discipline to practice, and an obsessive commitment to improve. But there was a small problem: I wasn't improving. For a few years, I remained at a standstill despite the endless hours I put in practicing. I was putting in the practice time required to get better, but the way I was practicing—the specific things I did—wasn't moving me forward. What little progress I was making (and it was little) was far from commensurate with the time I was devoting to it. I was guilty of bad busy with good intent.

I didn't get any better until I hired a professional who taught me how to improve. This enabled me to convert my practice from bad busy with good intent to good busy with good intent. I was now busy in a purposeful way, focusing on improving the specific mechanical flaws in my swing. Further, I was making progress at a faster pace while spending less time practicing.

If we choose to look closely, most of us will find endless examples of this dynamic infecting our personal and professional lives. Take fitness, for example. Between the years of 2002 and 2012, I was going to the gym three to four times a week. Yet somehow I managed to look worse with each passing year. My body got softer; my waist expanded. How was that possible? Well, I was bad busy with good intent. It was good that I was exercising, but I wasn't exercising in a purposeful way. Rather, I was going through the same tired routine week after week, month after month, year after year. And importantly, as I explore more specifically in chapter 9, my nutrition wasn't aligned to support the bodily transformation I sought. After a decade of being stagnant and even regressing, I knew I had to make a change. Again, with the help of a professional, I was able to align my workouts and nutrition to optimize my effort. I became good busy and voila—I finally started to see results.

Good busy with good intent is the model way to process our lives. It's when we use effective methods to make steady progress toward articulated goals.

Here's one more example.

To optimize my clinical practice, I sought to find the most productive uses of my time while treating my patients to provide maximum value to them. I took a close look at my professional rituals and came up with a structure that allowed me to operate at peak productivity. Rather than seeing patients all day every day as most doctors do, I looked at the schedules in both of my offices to see when demands for appointments were the greatest. After identifying the patterns, I broke my patient-care hours into three- or four-hour blocks.

For example, in my New York City office, my patients prefer to be seen before work on Mondays. In my Long Island office, I see patients Monday evenings during a three-hour block because my patients there like to come in after work. Kids' appointment slots are after they get out of school. Friday mornings are special as well: I set aside a block of three hours in the morning to perform cosmetic procedures in my New York City office so patients can recover over the weekend. The same is true for when I read slides to diagnosis and analyze skin conditions, which I do first thing in the morning when my mind is sharpest for that activity.

Making this change in my schedule allowed me to spend fewer hours on patient care yet be more productive. Optimizing my workflow to be only good busy has helped me and my patients.

We maximize life processes and achieve peak productivity in direct proportion to how much we build on our strengths, lessen our limitations, and are most efficient in performing tasks that bring value to those around us. This is the essence of purposeful practice and being good busy—the keys to optimizing our potential. We end up where we belong because we are both the navigator and the driver in this journey.

2

Core Values: The Foundation

*"It's not hard to make decisions once
you know what your values are."*

—ROY DISNEY

A recurring theme in this book is the amazing dividends we get from taking a clear and honest look at ourselves. There is so much to gain by peering inside to know who we are and what values define us—with that insight, we can then shape the path that will take us where we have the potential to go. To me, this is "keeping it real." Others may see it as a form of mindfulness. Others may prefer to call it conscious living.

Labels aside, the journey to finding our true self begins with articulating our core values, or the principles that identify what is important to us, define who we are and what we're about, and use where we've already been to help us get where we're going.

On a personal level, core values are guideposts for how we conduct our lives and align our internal and external worlds. Defining our core values allows us to organize our thoughts and actions in a way that empowers us to achieve our ambitions. It also helps us make decisions and troubleshoot mishaps.

In business and professional settings, core values shape an organization's culture and fuel the advancement of strategic visions.

In all cases, core values are timeless and enduring. That's not to say they can never change—they can and should as we learn and evolve. But at whatever place we occupy at a given time in our lives, our constant goal should be to identify three or four values that feed everything we do.

Like so many of us, for a long time I didn't pay much attention to core values or think about what mine were or could or should be, certainly not in a conscientious way. I did what I did every day, often based on habit or out of instinct. I didn't realize that most of my decisions, interactions, and actions reflected values I hadn't spelled out in any considered way. I hadn't stepped back to appreciate and understand how these values meshed with behavior and decision-making, and how, from that perspective, I was showing up in the world.

Then someone introduced me to a business book by Gino Wickman titled *Traction*, which opened me to an entirely different vantage point. *Traction* explored values in a way that captured my attention. Wickman argues—urges, really—that we're missing out if we don't thoughtfully articulate the values that matter the most to us, not only in connection with what we do professionally but also in our everyday personal lives. I came away from the book with a deeper appreciation for how well-defined and well-understood core values are transformative and provide a foundation for how to live a more successful and fulfilling life.

Taking a cue from the book, I compiled a short list of my personal core values, mindful that no formula existed and that whatever list I came up with could be shorter or longer or the same or different than anyone else's. Core values, I knew, aren't preordained or plucked off the shelf like a one-size-fits-all garment. They're customized for each of us.

I challenged myself to sense what resonated with me the most regarding lifestyle and decision-making and how I interacted with people both socially and professionally. I asked myself various questions. What behavior of mine did I like or, even better, felt most proud of? What behavior did I not like and could do without? What was missing in how I made decisions? What habits of mine seemed out of sync with who I thought I was or what I wanted to achieve? What was working well for me, and why?

This became a deeply introspective process that brought me up close and personal with who I aspired to be and what principles I wanted to govern my life. I was trying to determine what I stood for on a fundamental level—no small task for anyone, but so worthwhile.

It was an eye-opening exercise that forced me to come to terms with everything in my life: how I related to family and friends, how I ran my dermatology practice and dealt with patients, and how, in that mix, I could prioritize the values I wanted to hold near and dear. I wound up identifying four core values as the moral hub for my personal and professional life. They are care and compassion, integrity, accountability, and attention to detail. These four values serve as sources of wisdom and inspiration to draw upon and keep me on track.

Care and Compassion

For me, care and compassion are in the same group of emotions and values that includes empathy, kindness, and dignity. Together, they are the feelings I want to express to whoever I encounter, applying the same heartfelt spirit I show loved ones or close friends and colleagues.

I don't mean to suggest that the depth and range of care and compassion I want to impart can or should be the same for everyone. Personal intimacy and the depth of connection in relationships can of course vary widely. I'm talking about basic human decency in the larger sense—a mindset that engages people with respect and in a manner that recognizes and affirms them, whether dealing with strangers, a customer or patient, a UPS delivery person, or a checkout clerk at the market.

To be sure, this isn't always easy, especially if you live a hectic, dot-to-dot life where your to-do list never ends and you labor under pressure or stress. Chaotic lives distract and preoccupy us, making it difficult to allocate time to focus on meaningful connections.

But think about it. We have literally countless opportunities to encounter others each day and extend genuinely good vibes. It often doesn't take much, and how we handle those experiences reflects our values and priorities. These moments, even the most fleeting of them, give us the chance to connect with others in an uplifting way, whether with a quick smile, an encouraging or friendly glance, or a genuine thank-you. Leading with care and compassion to recognize the humanity of others and show an interest in them without judgment is essential to me. This simply means spreading good karma and abiding by the golden rule.

The potential far-reaching impact that a small morsel of positivity can have is astounding. I know this firsthand from what I've been blessed to receive during my professional career. I keep each thank-you card and kind note I've received from my patients and students. On those tough days, which we all have, I draw on their content for a needed boost. I will be forever grateful for and inspired by the care and compassion others have shown me.

Integrity

Selecting integrity as an essential value may seem self-evident to most, and hopefully it is, but unfortunately it increasingly seems to get lost in the chaotic shuffle of our world. From my perspective, integrity is the glue of a thriving and evolving culture. It's synonymous with a strong moral compass, and it entails approaching everyone with the same baseline of respect.

Integrity means keeping our word—both to ourselves and to others—and aligning our actions with our truth. We can't pick and choose when to be in integrity and when to take the easy, habitual, or less confrontational way. When integrity is ignored, we suffer as a community and as a species. When integrity is honored, we celebrate humanity.

Integrity is a broad term that manifests in numerous ways. In the workplace, it means completing your job honestly and to the best of your ability. I've too often seen people skate by or leave their tasks unfinished because they assume or wish that someone else will pick up the slack for the greater good of the team. Being part of a team means you know your role and fulfill it to the best of your ability—that's the essence of being a team player. In contrast, leaving your partners or colleagues to clean up the mess you leave behind shows a lack of integrity.

I'll share another example from my professional life.

In my dermatology practice, it isn't uncommon for me to turn away patients seeking cosmetic procedures, not because I don't want to serve them, but because they sometimes request a procedure that in my professional judgment won't achieve the results they seek or that they may later regret. For me, it isn't about making a quick buck or an easy sale; it's about going to sleep at night knowing I was honest and did what I believed was right for my patients. Turning a patient away—which for some may be a counterintuitive business practice—isn't easy. After all, in most cases the patient will seek treatment (and spend their money) elsewhere. But acting out of integrity, regardless of what angst it produces, is the right play, and one that provides life-affirming value you can't put a price tag on.

Integrity and accountability (my next core value I discuss) are intimately intertwined. This is a lesson I learned the hard way when I was about ten years old.

My best friend at the time, Steve Burr, invited me to attend an Iona College basketball game with him and his dad, who was an alumnus and huge fan of their basketball program. I was honored to be asked. Comparing my life to Steve's, we had what seemed polar opposite existences. He enjoyed a traditional nuclear family. His dad was a high school teacher and his mom a nurse. Steve was hugely popular in school, a good looking, blond-haired, blue-eyed kid who excelled at sports and dressed nicely, and even wore Nike sneakers. His dad played sports with him, he participated in soccer and little league, and he had a basketball hoop at home. And, his family gathered as a unit each night at the dinner table. To my eye, he had a textbook American life.

I had never been to a live sporting event and was super-excited for the chance to do so. On the day of the game, however, tempted by an alternate social opportunity, I flaked on Steve and, worse, his dad. At the time, I didn't think it was a big deal; after all Steve and his dad would go to the game regardless. But when I learned later how disappointed Steve's dad was with me, my heart dropped deep into my stomach. Worse, years later, when I'd be home from college and run into Mr. Burr in the neighborhood, he would casually bring it up. Even now, when I think about the poor judgement I exercised that day and how I let Mr. Burr down, my heart sinks. I learned there is little more important in life than keeping my word (integrity), and I vowed always to hold myself to a higher standard when it comes to doing so (accountability).

Accountability

We all have flaws. We all make mistakes. We all fail. I've certainly stumbled my fair share of times; it's to be expected and, in some cases, desired. As discussed in chapter 8, failing is the "life hiccup" that makes us human and allows us to see the nuances in our lives and learn what to fix, what to maintain, and what to leave behind.

When we err, accountability is next in the lineup. It directs us to come to terms with ourselves and figure out what went awry—and, most importantly, why. Accountability nurtures success. It allows us to take steps to understand our mistakes and craft responses that eliminate or minimize them in the future. When we make the same mistakes repeatedly, we fool ourselves and don't grow. Not having accountability means we don't care. If we don't care, we don't grow. If we don't grow, we don't succeed.

Accountability is liberating.

For me, accountability has meant bagging my excuses—I've learned that, as convenient as they can be, they get me nowhere. It's a cop-out to say things like, "Hey, you know what? I'm not smart enough to do this," or, "I'm not fit enough to do that," or, "My parents didn't have enough money to get me what I need." Wallowing in such indulgences is a one-way ticket to sustained failure. Blaming others is cheap and easy, a surefire way to stay stagnant. Survival and success mean getting over setbacks, owning mistakes, and coming up with fixes to move forward and achieve goals.

For example, if you want to get in shape, like I did, but you find yourself eating foods or exercising in a way that undermines your goal, like I did, the fix begins when you find the self-awareness and honesty to call yourself on it.

We must ask the tough questions. What is it about my life that enabled me to do that? How can I prevent it from happening again?

Similarly, the value of surrounding ourselves with people who hold us accountable, and avoiding those who don't, can't be overstated. Look to those who can help and guide you and drop those who enable success-killing behavior. We all need support systems and checks and balances. I know because that's exactly what I needed to begin making progress toward my goals. Tough love is hard to swallow, but it's an elixir for growth.

The ability to admit error and absorb the consequences head-on frees us. When errors occur, the commitment to figuring out what happened, and why, is what separates those who spin their wheels and stay stagnant from those who grab the wheel and drive steadily toward their ambitions. Little is more rewarding than solving what caused the mistake. Yes, it takes courage and self-assurance. But once accountability becomes an ingrained habit, it opens the gateway to turning failure into growth. That is what "fail your way to success" actually means—failing, then making an adjustment to overcome what caused you to fail. That's progress!

Attention to Detail

When it comes to my own personal and professional growth, I consider attention to detail critical. To me, it's what separates bad from mediocre, mediocre from good, good from very good, and very good from excellent. The elite performers, be they actors, scientists, athletes, or other professionals, pay keen attention to the little things, looking for precision in their execution and respecting nuances. It's a mindset that limits error, inspires confidence, builds reputation and credibility, and produces a high quality of life. It shows us that we're reliable and that we care about what we do and who we are.

Attention to detail is the X factor.

This fineness of focus may seem obvious for someone in a dermatology practice, and it plays a big role in how one conducts examinations, performs surgery, or administers a cosmetic procedure. But it goes far beyond that.

Attention to detail is just what it says it is: being truly mindful of every single detail. In my medical practice, this means paying attention to the entire patient experience.

Yes, when I'm in the exam room with my patient, I'm in full control and can curate their encounter. But the patient experience extends far beyond the exam room. How are they greeted when they call the office? Are they met with a smile when they enter the office? Are they offered a bottle of water while they wait? Are we doing everything possible to operate on schedule? Are we contacting patients with laboratory results in a timely manner? Attention to detail applies to every facet of what I do, whether I'm directly involved or in the background.

On a personal level, if I want to stay in sound physical condition, am I being attentive to each detail of what I'm putting into my system? Am I making sure I'm getting the necessary doses of carbohydrates, protein, and fat (macronutrients)? Truthfully, I didn't make any real progress toward my fitness goals until I weighed my food and beverages (yes, on a scale!) and documented each ounce that went into my body. A seemingly insane level of attention to detail is what it took for me. Yes, it may seem like that borders on obsessive-compulsive behavior, but the hard truth is, it's the type of commitment required to effect real, sustainable change. It's all about executing at the micro level.

Look at any of the greats and you'll see this same pattern of obsessive behavior. Kobe Bryant, one of the greatest NBA players of all time, famously wouldn't stop practicing until he made four hundred shots! Michael Jordan, Serena Williams, and Tiger Woods had similar detail-oriented compulsions that allowed them to become the best of the best.

Values have many sources. Some may have been instilled by parents, schools, or other external influences. Some may be the product of long-term experience. Others may originate within us. Values can be shared, similar, or different among family members, friends, and colleagues.

The list of possible core values is in the hundreds, and they run the gamut of the human experience. Besides the ones I've mentioned, they can include things like loyalty, commitment, intelligence, open-mindedness, courage, truth, innovation, friendship, perseverance, fitness, education, transparency, spirituality, respect, gratitude, valor, service to others, and environmentalism, to provide but a sampling.

Whatever their sources and however long the list of options, think about identifying the values that work best for you and say the most about you. This exercise has two parts. First, identify the values reflected in your past as well as in your current behavior and decision-making. The second is to identify the values you want to govern your life moving forward—your vision of the future.

Looking in the mirror of the present, how do you normally behave in a crunch, when you're emotionally and mentally tested? What do you do when push comes to shove? What provokes you the most, whether in a good or bad way? What disappoints you the most? What makes you feel the proudest? What gives you the most joy or meaning? What traits do you admire in others? Finally, how should you prioritize your short list of values?

Identifying our core values comes with many rewards, but going deep inside ourselves may challenge convenient self-perceptions or assumptions about ourselves that we're instinctively disinclined to disturb. We may not be 100 percent honest the first time around. But if we stay committed to the task with candor and courage, returning again and again until we widen the aperture of our internal evaluation, we'll produce a value-based foundation that will last a long time.

Defining your core values is an essential tool that will help you get closer to the greatness within; I know it's certainly helped me. Taking the time to do this with self-honesty—and taking the plunge into a principle-based life—can be a joyful awakening.

3

Empowerment

*"Whether you think you can,
or you think you can't—you're right."*

—HENRY FORD

When I escaped the uninspired monotony of my hamster-wheel life, I brought with me an essential insight: if I could do it, anyone could. I know it sounds like a cliché; the kind of comment that draws a response like, "Easy for you to say." But this sentiment struck me at my core as a profound and universal truth and opened me up to understanding more clearly that, fundamentally, anyone can transform themselves.

Everyone's methods, styles, values, and roads to success will differ, just like our individual definitions of success itself (as explored in chapter 10). But I've learned that the ultimate prizes are out there for whoever commits to pursuing them. Yes, it will take a shit ton of work, effort, and grit, but these are all free and accessible to anyone who has the guts to believe in themselves and the fortitude to grind toward their goals, however they define them.

Little saddens me more than seeing someone who, for whatever reason, is unable or unwilling to exploit their unused potential. We each possess value. We each bring something special to the table. We each have the power within waiting to be ignited. The question is, are we opening the doors of opportunity around us by exploring our vast potential? Or are we closing them by choosing the path of least resistance, the status quo?

The power that drives us to success springs from a genuine belief in ourselves—an unwavering, even primal, internal feeling that whatever our goals are, no matter how steep the mountains we face, no matter what obstacles we encounter along the way, if we put the work in, hustle and grind, and are unwavering in our commitment, we will achieve what we set out to accomplish. Without an unyielding, strong belief in ourselves that yes, we can actually do it, we have virtually nothing to do but spin our wheels, or even worse, go backward, leaving our vast potential to rot away.

While self-belief is the engine, it doesn't roar into full gear automatically. It doesn't have a switch we can flip on at will. It requires healthy and steady doses of self-candor, or internal transparency. Before we can believe in ourselves, we must know ourselves intimately, with all the good and all the flaws. Looking in the mirror and seeing the layers and nuances is the first step to aligning who we are with our actions and goals.

It can be hard to summon an unbiased vision of who we are. Nor is it easy to come to grips with and accept what we see when we take a deep look. But we have the means to get clear on it—if we dare. Deep and recurring introspection can bring the self-awareness and self-honesty vital to self-empowerment.

How many times have you taken a close look into yourself and said, Who do I see? What makes up the real me? What are my strengths and weaknesses? What are my personal flaws? Where do I need work and improvement? What makes me distinct? What am I capable of?

Our self-power lies in knowing how our essential character can best serve us, especially in areas where we're lacking. Shortcomings aren't necessarily a negative—it's all in how we choose to handle them. Personal weaknesses can be powerful tools that direct the adjustments we need to make to exercise power over our lives and enjoy a robust path to maximizing our potential. I love the saying "the obstacle is the way," based on a quote from Marcus Aurelius. Overcoming personal weaknesses is the path to self-empowerment.

Here is a personal example that I believe illustrates this point.

About a decade ago, a few buddies and I decided to go on a golf trip to Scottsdale, Arizona. Having barely touched a golf club before this trip, I was hands down the least talented of the group. I sprayed balls in every direction except straight, found hazards wherever they were (even behind me!), and lost at least a dozen golf balls per round. Clearly, the game of golf did not come easy to me; anyone could see that. In contrast, the rest of my group either had pre-existing skills or much more God-given talent than I had. Everything flowed naturally for them—they could navigate the course smoothly, with little effort and angst, as if they were playing a different game than I was. It didn't take long for me to realize that if I wanted to close the gap and keep pace with them and limit embarrassment, I had to come to grips with my shortcomings, not feel bad about them, and believe I could do something about them. Otherwise I'd be mired in mediocrity, a place I hated being.

To improve along the lines I wanted, I knew I had to go balls to the wall. I practiced week in and week out, including during the winter months. I received private instruction on the extensive weak aspects of my game through weekly golf lessons all year round, which I continue to this day. Not being a natural meant I needed to develop sound mechanics and good habits and employ the help of a professional to keep me on track. I also needed patience and a long-term vision. It was going to take years of work, week in and week out.

The process was slow and painful. To sustain this amount of effort, I needed to find value in the baby steps, as, over time, they lead to large strides. The importance of baby steps can't be overemphasized. They are the essence of what "trusting the process" means.

Each year, in barely discernible increments, I began to improve. Eventually, the consistency and accumulation of my improved performance caught the attention of the rest of my group. I'd caught up to them, and even surpassed some. They were taken aback that I could now compete and play consistently at their levels. I wasn't headed to the PGA Tour anytime soon, but I'd found a way—by embracing baby steps—to elevate my game, and I continued to get better each year by simply plugging away with purposeful practice.

I had faced my inherent weaknesses with a strong belief that I could address them effectively through hustle and grind. My golfing buddies, on the other hand, stayed flat during this same period. To be honest, none of them are as obsessive-compulsive as I am, and they probably couldn't care less about getting better at golf as much as I did and do. But they still didn't leverage their strengths the way I utilized my weaknesses. They plateaued and I, by being honest with myself and determined to improve, found a path to a higher level of performance. It was a small, yet valuable, lesson in transforming a personal limitation into a strength.

Many of us have had similar experiences in our lives where we've assessed which personal strengths to emphasize and which shortcomings to work on. It begins with self-honesty and having the courage to tackle change and engage the drive to be better that resides in all of us.

Some people struggle with finding and harnessing this power and often can't get on a track to steady growth. Laziness, which can sabotage a needed effort to do better, get better, and be better, plays a role in this, but a lack of self-belief is often the root cause. If we don't think we can do it, we can't.

Other factors play a role too, namely the lack of good habits and consistency. Habits are either our best friends or our worst enemies; they're either good or bad. The bad keep us down and in a rut. They dampen our spirit and, in the process, dilute our personal power and stifle our growth. The good, on the other hand, empower us, embolden us, and drive us forward.

I learned all this the hard way.

During what I call my "physical rut" period, my wife and I had our three beautiful children. As each child arrived, as happens to so many parents, my attention refocused away from me. I was tired all the time, I lost my zip, I drank too much beer and ate like shit, and I stopped exercising. These new bad habits conspired to add serious pounds to my body. Over the course of four to five years, I ballooned to almost two hundred pounds and my body fat catapulted to 21 percent. I had managed to add unsightly rolls to my midriff and become a soft and flabby guy; a skinny-fat dude with a big gut and man boobs. I knew my habits had to change.

During the peak of my physical decline, we moved to the suburbs, where I met Rahsaan Robinson, a highly regarded personal trainer. When Rahsaan asked me to state my goals, I told him, in rough terms, that I wanted to get "jacked and ripped." I wanted to transform my body, look good with my shirt off, and be in tip-top shape. Looking at the flabby specimen of a man standing in front of him, Rahsaan knew it would be an ambitious project, to say the least. Without missing a beat, he told me that, given where

I was and where I wanted to be, it would take three to five years of difficult work and I would need to develop the necessary consistent habits. This would be no easy thirty-day transformation like you see on TV!

I signed up. (A side bet with my brother-in-law helped fuel my ambition further.)

My workouts were consistent, and my diet was dialed in to the last macronutrient. I weighed my food and got up before sunrise to work out when needed. I lost forty pounds and reduced my body fat to 8 percent within six months. I worked my tail off, grinding day after day, week after week, month after month, and then year after year, with resolute consistency. I put in the time and effort, focused on each step, never looked past each day, and religiously honored my new habits. Baby steps led to massive change—I hit my short-term goals and pressed ahead. Now, more than seven years later, I have a body I'm proud of and I've set even higher physique goals for myself. The renewed grind continues.

Reaching a long-term goal is not the last lap. In fact, there is no last lap. You don't get into shape to get out of shape; when you hit a fitness goal, or any goal for that matter, it's critical to regroup and set a new, bigger goal for yourself. The cumulative effect of daily wins and achieving goals fuels enduring self-empowerment. This is precisely how we stretch the limits of our potential and grow to heights we never thought possible.

My habits had been consistently bad before, and now they're consistently good. With each workout, I'm invigorated and confident. My new habits are ingrained in my lifestyle, and I never miss a workout—even if it means hitting the gym at 4:30 AM. or while on vacation. The good habits I've developed empower me, and I hold myself accountable to them.

Of course, just as habits must be consistent, goals must be realistic. They shouldn't be all short-term or immediate, and they should fit within an overall strategy, which could mean that the goal is years away. Goals should be structured to yield a steady flow of modest accomplishments that build on each other. These are what I like to call tiny wins: modest achievements that are easily measured, fuel internal power, and instill greater self-confidence. You want a personal goal program that allows you to move incrementally forward to something larger each day or week. Find joy in each step, however small. Those small steps will lead to big results. Trust me.

Once your plan is in place, be accountable as you move toward your goals. Don't fool yourself—be brutally honest no matter how much it unsettles or frustrates you. If you're inattentive to the process or just pay lip service to it, or if your habits are inconsistent or you suffer more than a rare lapse, the first person who should be all over you for it is you. When it comes to a system of goals, be your own worst critic. Otherwise the entire process is a fool's errand, a colossal waste of time and, in some cases, money.

The flip side is identifying and isolating the bad habits that keep you inert and dilute your power. Never forget that you control your habits, both good and bad. Everyone stumbles and needs change here and there; it's part of the experience. The key is being self-aware enough to identify the routines that need fixing. Know and decisively eliminate the things holding you back so they don't recur. This is the essence of personal accountability, which is a vital component in achieving any goal.

Justin Jefferson, another fitness professional I work with, is fond of the saying, "The way you do anything is the way you do everything." I love that statement. When we're firing on all cylinders, it speaks to how consistency breeds excellence. When we aren't, it underscores the opposite and derails our forward progress. Consistent excellence across the board is a high bar, no doubt. It challenges even the most talented professional athletes. But it's a performance standard that keeps us honest and hungry; it's our guard against compromise and slippage. You can't be half-assed with some things and painstakingly attentive to detail with others—the way you do anything is really the way you do everything. Excellence in everything, every time, every day, should be the goal.

Beware the influences that threaten to zap your power. We all run into impediments in our personal quests that can undermine what we're trying to achieve. Few are as bad as people who cast shade or saturate us with negative energy. The same is true for those who are unwilling or unable to embrace you as you are and support you and your goals. The saying "haters gonna hate" is a fact of life.

When you begin to elevate your game, beware of those in your circle—including family members and longtime friends—who are threatened by your efforts toward self-improvement and personal growth. Hard as it may be, avoid situations with negative energy or people who seem more interested in bringing you down than raising you up. Too many people get in their own way and stifle their personal growth by hanging with the wrong crowd, an environment that can dilute confidence and reduce us to be lazy. Plain and simple, eliminate the haters from your circle. When it comes to your potential, you can either rise or fall, depending on the company you keep.

At times, I too have grappled with others' negativity. I remember when I first started posting to Instagram daily, before I'd built a sizeable platform. I posted a video about a local barbershop where my sons got their hair cut, called Izik's Barber Shop. I love that place. It has a hip urban vibe, the cuts are on point, and the fades are tight. More than that, Steve the barber is a meticulous master at what he does; an artist with shears and clippers. He uses his skills with care and precision, and I find the process fascinating. The haircuts take time—they test a kid's patience—but they're well worth the wait. It's a thrill to watch Steve perform his craft with such flair and pride.

So, one day I popped into Izik's unannounced with my videographer to surprise my boys as Steve was about to do his handiwork. I posted an amazing video, which to this day still brings a smile to my face, with my sons and the crew at Izik's. It's only a minute long, but it captures so much of what I love, particularly Steve's pride in his work, his unyielding attention to detail, and of course my beautiful boys.

After the video posted, the professional grapevine spawned some negative feedback. Why would a successful dermatologist post such a thing? Why was I putting myself out there like that? Wasn't I being a little weird, or less than professional?

Initially, I felt a little sting. I mean who likes to hear negative noise spewed behind their backs. Was my content out of line in some way? Was it unprofessional? Did I lack self-awareness?

The easy path was to be defensive; to drink from the cup of self-doubt and surrender to the negativity. But that would give others control and power over me. Conversely, I could reaffirm my belief in myself, redouble my commitment to an ambitious social media mission (to present an authentic and honest representation of myself and spread a message of positivity and self-empowerment), and forge ahead with greater resolve.

I chose the latter and ignored the haters. I became more fortified and confident, and my belief in myself and my mission skyrocketed. I took what could have been a downturn or reversal and turned it into fuel for what I wanted to do and what I wanted to accomplish. Choosing to ignore the trash-talking put me in a stronger and firmer position than ever before. It was an extraordinary, self-empowering revelation.

This experience reminded me how negativity can either be the poison of self-doubt or the catalyst for new and exciting opportunities. By choosing opportunity, I was able to convert negativity into a positive force and up the ante on my commitment. I believed in what I was doing and knew I had to resist the temptation to allow unfavorable reactions to throw me off course.

It came down to control. Some things we can control and some we can't. This was something I could control—and should. The goal is to identify and focus on what we can control and confidently take the wheel.

Fast forward to the present day and my professional colleagues, patients, friends, and strangers often tell me how much they enjoy what I'm putting out there on social media. Once considered out of the ordinary and even "weird" for a successful doctor, my content is now considered to be game-changing and inspirational. Some have even asked for my help with their own social media platforms—go figure!

I'm grateful for the chance to impact others positively, and I don't fault anyone for their prior criticisms. I understand that the world of social media was somewhat new and fast developing, particularly in a field like medicine. Old opinions die hard, but change is rife with opportunity. The secret sauce is authenticity.

Self-awareness, self-honesty, good habits, consistency, well-drawn goals, and trusting the process by letting small wins propel us forward are the fuel for self-belief and empowerment. There will always be a gap between performance and unfilled potential. The more we apply ourselves with fierce diligence, however, the more we narrow this gap, the more we can accomplish and enjoy. Our capacity to grow seems infinite or, at the very least, expandable. We'll always have new opportunities for fulfillment if we're open to continually exploring our potential.

Know and believe in yourself, trust your instincts, and feel the power.

4

The Value of Others

"A mentor is someone who sees more talent and ability within you than you see in yourself, and helps bring it out of you."

—BOB PROCTOR

A guest on my podcast once said, "Success leaves clues." The simple wisdom in these words is that we aren't in this alone. Far from it—we're blessed with abundant opportunities to learn from people who have done it before. Their success stories burst with valuable lessons learned, cutting-edge ideas, and time-tested techniques and methods.

The beauty is that today we don't need direct access to successful people to learn how they managed to conquer the mountains of their ambitions and ring the bells of their accomplishments. Think about a successful person you admire. Have they chronicled their journeys in a memoir? Are audio interviews with them available in podcasts or other formats? Do they speak at conferences or conduct online webinars, workshops, or lectures? Can you find them on YouTube holding forth on something that speaks to you?

The explosion of social media, documentaries, and memoirs has made it easy for us to learn and borrow from an array of people who have blazed paths to success. It's all there for us—if we want it. It can be a classic rags-to-riches story or a tale about how a successful person survived a horrendous upbringing that inspires you to wonder what you can do with similar focus and drive. Maybe it's a how-to book that shares a simple formula or precise tools to address certain life situations, or a memoir that changes the way you think about yourself and your life. Perhaps it's a documentary on how a plant-based diet can change your life in ways you'd never imagined, or a TED Talk that inspires you to take up a cause. Maybe it's a book like this that opens your eyes to the simple things you can do to get on track toward success and convinces you that you, too, can do it.

The bottom line is, be a sponge. We're surrounded by valuable life lessons and the clues of success.

No one gets to the top of their craft or achieves measurable life goals without the influence, inspiration, and assistance of others. Students have teachers. Athletes have trainers and coaches. Actors have drama teachers, agents, directors, and fellow actors to drive them to do their best. Workers in the trades have to apprentice, as do public servants. Artists have the vast influence of artists before them to influence their style. The list is endless.

The legendary basketball coach John Wooden once said, "It's what we learn after we know it all that counts." We can all benefit from that wisdom. There's always more to be learned, and in nearly all cases, there's someone out there we can learn from.

I appreciate the instinct to resist the temptation to copy others—it's natural to want to do things by ourselves so we can earn the right to say we did it our way, on our own. To some extent, this is admirable. It shows the resolve and industry needed to be successful and continue to grow. But looking to others for ways to help us succeed, and even doing some copying along the way, isn't inconsistent with having the hustle and grind to pave our own path; it's just another way of taking control of our destiny. Emulating others and taking initiative operate synergistically: using lessons from those who've done it before and adding our unique "flavor" to our approach can produce huge results.

When we look to others for ideas, influence, and inspiration, the task is to identify what's useful and makes the most sense for us, and then adapt what we learn to our style and way of doing things. This won't be the same for everyone—we each have our own way of learning and expressing ourselves, and we need our own customized processes.

In pursuing most any goal, many of the components of our success are derived from others. The remainder reflect our unique imprint. Take, for instance, a golf swing. Virtually all professional golfers have a swing that appears identical at impact (i.e., where the ball is hit, which is the critical part of the swing). But what happens before or after this impact differs between golfers, and this is where that ever-important individual stamp is found. The "business" part of the swing is identical for professional golfers, while the "non-business" part of the swing is unique—just as the "business" part of achieving a goal is often similar from person to person while the "non-business" part is distinct.

Going beyond the relative ease of finding inspiration among the celebrated and publicly visible, we also have access to the people whose paths we cross in our daily lives. The first tier of influence, apart from our parents, are our mentors and role models. Over a lifetime, we're blessed if we can count among our benefactors even a handful of people who took us under their wing at different times and showered us with sage advice and ideas, whether by example, wonderfully expressed words, passionate or provocative teaching, or a healthy combination of all of the above.

Role models come in all styles, and sometimes when we least expect them. Be alert to what they can teach you. Have no shame in absorbing their wisdom. Mimicking the traits of role models and allowing them to impact you are essential ingredients for success, not only during the earlier stages of our lives when we're trying to find our way, but later when we're stuck in our ways and, well, think we know it all.

Sometimes, the impact of a mentor is felt many years after the mentoring experience. That happened to me.

One of my earliest role models other than my mom was my fifth-grade teacher, Mr. McCarthy. He must have been close to seventy years old at the time. He was a kind and gentle man who quickly became one of my favorite teachers. My fondest memory of him had to do with a magic trick he performed before major school recesses like Christmas or Easter. The magic performance was his way of keeping our attention fresh and breaking up the day with a little entertainment, and it captivated the class, as it certainly did me. While too young to appreciate the clever teaching method, I was taken with his command of the room and the absolute mystery of what he seemed to pull off.

The trick seemed simple on the surface. Mr. McCarthy had three tools: a paper bag, handwritten notes from his students, and his mind. First, he directed each student to write a message on a piece of paper, fold the paper up, and put it in the paper bag. Then he reached into the bag, removed one of the folded pieces of paper, pressed it against his temple, and, using claimed "ESP," predicted what it said. After getting the first one correct, he would pull out the next piece of paper and repeat the exercise, which he continued to do over and over again, with unflinching success, hitting the jackpot each time without fail. We were flabbergasted. It was magic!

The first time I saw the trick, I couldn't imagine how he'd done it even once, never mind consistently, with such uncanny accuracy. I thought he had a gift. I soon realized, however, that there *had* to be a trick, and I was determined to figure it out. At first, I didn't know where to start. To my preteen mind, the trick defied logic; I began to think that maybe, just maybe, Mr. McCarthy really did have telepathic powers, and that magic was real. I enlisted the help of my older brother, several years my senior, and we suffered a tiring series of trial and error until the light went on and I cracked the code.

Now it seems so plain. Mr. McCarthy started off by predicting something that at least one of us would write. If, for instance, he performed the trick before Thanksgiving, he would start with, "I think this note says, 'Happy Thanksgiving.' Did anyone write down 'Happy Thanksgiving'?" Of course, at least one student had, and at least one enthusiastic hand would shoot up to say, "That was me!" Once Mr. McCarthy got this affirmation, he would open the note and, without showing it to us, tell the class that's what it said (even though it likely didn't). So far, so good.

For step two, he would reach back into the bag, pull out a second note, hold it to his temple, and recite what was written. Keep in mind that he never showed us what was written on the first, now discarded, note. For instance, if the first note said, "I love the Giants," he would now announce, "I think this (second) note says 'I love the Giants.' Did anyone write that?" And onward he would go, gaming the system and producing a perfect prediction each time.

When we returned to school after the break, I pushed out my little chest and proudly told Mr. McCarthy that I'd figured out his magic trick. He gave me an amused look and nodded. I explained the details of what I'd uncovered and got a pat on the back. He asked me to keep my discovery under my hat, however, and I did. The next time he prepared to do the trick for the class, toward the end of the year, he summoned me to the front of the room and asked that I assist him. He gave no advance warning—it was a command performance on call. I was confident; I hadn't forgotten.

It went beautifully. We worked together as if we were longstanding stage partners. I was enormously pleased with myself and imagined that I was the envy of the entire class. I'd gotten Mr. McCarthy's stamp of approval.

On the last day of school, as I walked out of the building thinking about the summer, Mr. McCarthy pulled me aside gently by the arm. I looked up at him eagerly, not sure what to make of his attention. He looked me dead in the eyes and said, "You *will* succeed." He made no other comment; he let go of my arm and walked away. I stood there smiling from ear to ear, although the full weight of those words didn't hit me until much later in my life.

That simple phrase—"you *will* succeed"—gave me the boost of a lifetime. To have someone believe in me that way, especially someone I held in high regard, and provide such a strong affirmation about what I could do in life was more than uplifting. It was sheer joy. That it occurred during a time when I was struggling socially, getting bullied non-stop, and managing to get embroiled in fights with peers was all the better. When I heard those words, a flame burst forth in my soul. Up until that point in my brief life, it was the most significant positive thing to happen to me.

The magic-trick experience taught me, in a small way, that I could do this. I could succeed in life. While my share of setbacks awaited me, that moment—how Mr. McCarthy looked me in the eyes with genuineness and care—has stayed with me and given me a boost during the tougher times in my life. I wish he were still alive so I could show him the positive, enduring impact of the three words he spoke to that insecure ten-year-old.

It took me awhile to put that fifth-grade experience into proper perspective, to understand its full meaning and how it benefited me.

Fundamentally, it taught me the value of mentors and role models. I eventually saw how important it was for someone I looked up to show belief in me. When people we admire and trust hold us up as knowledgeable, wise, and competent, the result is empowering. I also learned the value of learning life lessons from people beyond my family members. Sure, teachers are supposed to do that, but it doesn't always happen.

I also learned the importance of initiative, effort, and taking risks. Yes, attempting to figure out the magic trick was a playful exercise, but I could've failed, which would've forced me to admit to myself and my brother that I couldn't figure it out, and that the bravado I'd exhibited in thinking I could had been misplaced.

Finally, Mr. McCarthy taught me the value of drawing on others' skill sets. Learning his magic trick was a success in itself. I mimicked him—I did what he did, no more and no less, and it brought me success.

In this context, a couple of similar key moments in my life come to mind.

Dr. David Kriegel, one of my mentors during medical school, was a major reason why I completed my dermatology residency at Mount Sinai Hospital in Manhattan. Dr. Kriegel was a young skin-cancer surgeon who practiced in New York City and held teaching positions at both Mount Sinai and Stony Brook University, where I was a medical student. Because he wasn't that much older than the students and resident physicians he was training, Dr. Kriegel was the only attending physician up until that point who could engage us on both a professional level as students and a personal level as friends. Since I was hoping to pursue a career in dermatology, I couldn't have had a better person to emulate. Not only did he teach me a lot about dermatology, he also schooled me in how to conduct myself as a professional, have good bedside manner, be collegial, and mentor others.

At the end of each academic year during our Mount Sinai residency, each resident took a national exam designed to assess our preparedness for board certification and rank us nationally by specialty. I scored in the 76th percentile after my first year, which was among the highest scores in my residency group. I was satisfied, particularly because the dermatology residents' test scores were typically the highest compared to students in other specialties. If I was in the top 25 percent of this elite group, I was in pretty good shape.

When Dr. Kriegel learned of my score, however, instead of giving me the high five I was eagerly expecting, he said, "That's it?" His genuine disappointment took my breath away. I mean, it wasn't a bad score, and compared to my Mount Sinai peers, it was damn good. But after looking at the matter from his perspective, I could see that I was his guy in the residency program. He'd vouched for me during the admissions process, and my performance reflected directly on him. He was accustomed to me crushing exams at Stony Brook, and his reasonable expectation was that I would perform at the same elite level as a resident.

Those words—"that's it?"—were all I needed to elevate my game. I scored in the 99th percentile each year thereafter. I didn't do it for him; I did it because someone I admired and whose standards of performance I valued believed I could perform better. It was another wake-up call. His belief in me and my potential incited me to want more from myself and empowered me to get it done.

Another wonderful mentor I had was Dr. Ed Heilman, who, like me, is a dermatologist and dermatopathologist. I worked closely with Dr. Heilman during my fellowship year, when he was one of my supervising doctors, and the following year when he hired me to work in his laboratory. As is customary when you first start practicing, I leaned on him frequently, picking his brain as often as I could for his opinion on the slides I was reviewing. One day when I walked into his office, I found him hemming and hawing over a diagnosis in one of his cases. I sat down at the opposing end of the two-headed microscope and peered at the tissue he was reviewing. I noticed a subtle finding and said it could indicate a somewhat obscure diagnosis. Dr. Heilman peered over the microscope—all I saw were his eyes and the top third of his head—and said, "I've succeeded. The student has surpassed the teacher."

Wow! What stronger words of encouragement could a young doctor possibly hear? Dr. Heilman's kind and generous words gave me the confidence to believe I had the goods to be a great dermatopathologist. I will be forever grateful to him for that.

Three small phrases from three different individuals during three distinct periods of my life continue to impact me many years after the words were spoken: "You *will* succeed," "That's it?" and, "I've succeeded. The student has surpassed the teacher." You can also throw in what my friend Sami Khan said when I was at Emory: "Why don't you just try?"

Once again, mentors come in various forms and present themselves during different life stages. Sometimes their impact doesn't manifest immediately, but many years later.

When I reflect on all this, I distill the specific impact my mentors had on me to how they each objectively saw more potential in me than I did in myself, and how their declared belief in me drove me to grind harder and push myself further. I couldn't be more grateful to them. I'm certain that more mentors are in the wings; when our radar is on, they're all around us. They could be a friend, colleague, student, employee, or even one of our children. Our job is to keep our eyes, ears, and hearts open and our minds receptive.

5

It's All About Execution

"Execution is the game."
—GARY VAYNERCHUK

Achieving a personal goal can be marked by many things. It could be a trophy, a professional license, a diploma or other certificate worth framing, the number of pounds lost, a coveted grade on a test, reaching the summit of a steep mountain, the conditioning or sculpting of an out-of-shape body, a work promotion, a professional award, and on and on. In all instances, the achievement deserves celebration, provides bragging rights, and can be a deep source of pride.

More importantly, in many instances, the *act* of achieving is what inspires bigger and better pursuits.

Despite the well-deserved luster, an achieved goal is a product; a result of the accumulation and expression of a more fundamental success that precedes it. More than the goal itself, what endures and redefines us is what happens on the challenging road to our goals. Staying in the game until the very end is the most significant accomplishment.

That process of accomplishment is displayed in the habits we develop and the single-mindedness and specific purpose we bring en route to where we want to go. It's what happens when we embrace the hustle and grind of the small and sometimes difficult steps that snowball into greater things over time. It's what gives life to the principle that the cumulative result of small actions over time can be massive if we stick to the plan.

This is why, for me, it's all about execution and trusting and loving the process.

Once we have a well-devised game plan and have set ourselves in motion, our priorities should be to stay the course, believe deeply in the program we've outlined, have faith in ourselves, and let it play out, whatever comes.

Trusting the process is the most reliable guarantee that we will get results.

This doesn't mean we can't or shouldn't adjust and readjust on the journey. We need to be smart about the process and learn what works, what doesn't, and why. Success is reflected in how well we manage the steps we've mapped out to get to our goals, including what detours we choose to take. Failures can require an audible, which means renewed opportunities. As discussed in chapter 8, we shouldn't shy away from them; we should embrace them and make them agents of change for us.

Bring on the adversity. Bring on the missteps. Bring on whatever will test us and make us stronger and more confident. Failing is fine; not failing because we haven't tested the waters is not fine. The road to our goals is filled with learning opportunities whenever we embark boldly.

Keep in mind, too, that it's not what we do here and there that makes the difference. It's what we do day in, day out—the habits we develop and the well-considered routines we use, with their give and take, ups and downs, refinements and adjustments. These consistent patterns yield the results we feel great about. Make each moment count and be true to your plan, never losing sight of the reality that no plan is without flaws and no process is without hiccups. The imperfect process, with all its warts and splendor, is where genuine success is found.

If you want meaningful and sustainable results, don't dodge the individual meaningful steps to the goal. Dispense with shortcuts and hacks, as they prevent the development of good habits and mental discipline and sabotage your sustained success. As Michael Jordan said, "I've been taking shortcuts, yet I'm expecting the same results. It can't happen that way."

For instance, CliffsNotes may get you the information you need to write that paper, but you'll get nowhere near the same value you'd get from reading the actual book. Fat-burning supplements may get your heart rate up and help you burn a few more calories during your workout, but they'll always be significantly inferior to a disciplined diet and exercise regimen. The "grind" in hustle and grind is where you learn the lessons that reprogram your neurons with the success code. Shortcuts deprive you of learning these lessons and leave you treading water.

The success you think you've achieved by leapfrogging the long-term process and not doing the work is like finding fool's gold. When you look closely, you've achieved nothing except feeling a false sense of accomplishment to whet the ego.

Sustainable success means developing good habits that are sourced from the little things—those tiny wins. Those small steps, which alone seem inconsequential, are what fuel growth, keep the process moving, and build confidence when they're embraced and honored on a regular basis. They are the building blocks of your future.

Actor and rapper Will Smith expresses the concept this way: "You don't set out to build a wall. You don't say, 'I'm going to build the biggest, baddest, greatest wall that's ever been built.' You don't start there. You say, 'I'm going to lay this brick as perfectly as a brick can be laid.' You do that every single day. And soon you have a wall."

It's the perfectly executed little steps, with painstaking attention to detail, that accumulate slowly over weeks, months, or even years and lead to massive results.

We all take the bypass route sometimes. In certain circumstances, they're efficient. For instance, I deem it acceptable to drink a protein shake to meet my protein requirement for the day if I can't eat a meal. These things have no useful place, however, when we're seeking to achieve important life goals, or when we're trying to grow and develop who we are. Sure, it's tempting to get something done before its time. But when we focus in that way, we elevate expedience and comfort over long-term meaningful gain.

Our temptation to take shortcuts won't disappear—it lurks inside us. Almost every day, we're tempted to avoid the longer, more difficult road. Our task is to minimize or, better still, reject shortcuts entirely. The internal discipline that rejects a shortcut is the same discipline that forms the foundation for all good habits.

Take dieting, for example. The thirty-day, cure-all diets we see advertised time and again are enticing to a broad audience. But they're illusions and—sometimes harmful—distractions. They do not and cannot build good habits, which means they're fast tracks to nowhere. If you want to change your body and become healthier, you need a sustained lifestyle change steeped in exercise, eating, and other habits that will serve you for the rest of your life. Crash courses will do just that: crash you. And, to be sure, they will not change you.

To change my physique, it was essential for me to trust that getting a workout in on a firm schedule and meeting my daily nutrition goals would ultimately lead to the results I was hoping to achieve. When I started my private dermatology practice in New York City, I had to trust that my delivery of the best possible care to each of my first patients would yield sustained organic growth. When I started my social media efforts in earnest, it was critical for me to trust that posting to Instagram each day without exception would lead to increased awareness of my personal brand.

It all starts with setting a goal (e.g., getting in shape, building a successful dermatology practice, or increasing brand awareness on social media), and doing one thing each day to bring you closer to achieving it, no matter what. Your commitment should be at the level where not a day goes by when you don't do one thing to move the needle. This is what I mean by trusting the process and embracing the grind. Be thoughtful about your effort and process. Be accountable. Challenge yourself. That's how you execute.

I'll be the first to admit that the mental focus required to find value and joy in each tiny aspect of the goal-achievement process isn't easy. The ability to see every detail so that the smallest of them become all-encompassing in our focus requires mental discipline that most of us have to work steadily at developing. It takes time. It requires patience. It tests commitment. It's a habit in itself.

Consider weightlifting, for example. If you're lifting a barbell for a set of twelve repetitions, how often do you think, "I only have a few left," or, "The twelfth lift can't come fast enough?" How often do you turn your mental attention away from each repetition while you're doing it, half-assing it to get it done?

The gold standard is performing each rep with a technique designed to maximize its individual value. If your mind slips away from the technique and you aren't fully engaged in each rep, you're cheating yourself to some degree. You're missing out on the full benefit of the process and making it more difficult to build strong, self-sustaining habits. The mind–muscle connection is a real thing. Intensely focusing on the movement of the weight, one rep at a time, by connecting your mind and the muscle is the secret sauce to getting gains. Half-assed reps lead to half-assed results—a universal truth.

This is why so few make it to goals they're capable of achieving. It's not that the steps are beyond our ability to take; it's that they can be monotonous, boring, even mind-numbing. Going through them day after day, week after week, month after month is a sheer test of mental endurance. There will be days when we don't want to do the one thing we need to do. These are the days that differentiate success from failure and test our mental toughness. Giving in to the desire to take it easy or take one day off is a surefire way to undermine the pursuit of maximum success. Days off should be few and far in between. We may need to recharge now and then, but for the most part, the grind must be relentless. Even when I'm on vacation, I get workouts in, keep an eye on my business and my patients, and post to social media. As Dwayne "The Rock" Johnson loves to say, the key to his success is that he's the "hardest worker in the room." This Doc agrees—the difference makers are those who put in the work when others aren't willing to.

This applies to almost every endeavor we undertake, in every walk of life. A teacher who wants to serve their students well and help them become better citizens must fully commit to the lessons they're charged with teaching. They can't compromise for the sake of convenience or laziness. A successful businessperson can get lucky on occasion, but they can't afford to cut corners if they want to grow a sustainable company and create shareholder value. A professional athlete, no matter how naturally gifted they are, must mind the process in excruciating detail in order to move beyond competitors and achieve greatness.

We shouldn't discount the role that luck plays. I love the saying "the harder I work, the luckier I get." We each have various forms of luck that drop in our path at some point. What matters is how we capitalize on that luck when it arrives. It isn't surprising that one study claimed that nearly 70 percent of Florida lottery winners went broke within five years of winning a large purse. The hustle is what allows us to maximize these opportunities and double down on, rather than squander, a lucky break.

Just like tuning in to the small steps—each rep—of a workout is crucial to forming sustainable habits, small steps also develop the single-mindedness we need to accomplish our goals. Some people advocate becoming a multitasking master who juggles many activities at once to be successful. To them I say respectfully and in all candor: multitasking is bullshit.

When we multitask, we cheat ourselves and the people who rely on us. We can't perform at the high-quality levels we're capable of if our minds are engaged in split-screening. For example, if I'm performing a surgical procedure, I can't be thinking about who to include in my fantasy football roster. I'd be doing my patient a disservice and risking the quality of my work. If I'm in the gym pumping iron and I'm thinking about tomorrow's surgical procedures, I'd be doing my body a disservice. If my wife is speaking to me and I'm thinking about something in my medical practice or golf game, I'm not listening well and giving her the attention she deserves, I'm doing her (and us) a disservice.

Multitasking undermines execution. It splits and blurs the screens in our head and prevents us from being all in. When we aren't fully engaged, we cheat the process and ourselves. If we give one task attention at the expense of another, we deprive both of something. It's that simple.

That doesn't mean we can't do two things at once. People do that all the time, and sometimes they're even proud of their ability to juggle simultaneous activities. But here we're talking about a process designed to yield important personal results, not walking and chewing gum at the same time. We're talking about the kind of keen focus that will maximize personal potential and produce the best results. When placed in this all-important context, multi-tasking is your enemy. In contrast, consistent focus is your ally. It builds lasting good habits, improves the quality of your results, and provides confidence and momentum.

The quality of our effort goes hand in hand with mental discipline, which begins with embracing hard work as a good thing. It sounds simple; maybe too simple. Yet it often seems like we've lost sight of the value of good old-fashioned hard work—that nose-to-the-grindstone ethic that The Rock stressed earlier when talking about his own approach to his craft. From my vantage point, achieving the kind of change that will make a significant difference in your life, allowing you to find contentment and be fulfilled, requires a consistent, dialed-in effort.

That's what hustle and grind is about. Intense focus and single-mindedness are reflected in the full engagement of mind and body. Sure, you may limit the full intensity to short bursts of time, but the pattern must be there and the commitment can't waver. When you come to a crossroads, your choice must always be to forge ahead and not walk away, no matter how daunting the challenge or how hard you're tested.

It's not merely hard work that's essential. We need to work hard *and* work smart.

I wrote earlier about "good busy" and the lasting lessons I learned in developing my golf game. I'd spent countless hours working hard, but without knowing how to improve. I was putting in the time; I was working very hard. But the results I expected from my efforts weren't coming. I didn't realize it at the time, but I wasn't working smart. It wasn't until I got professional advice on what I needed to learn and focused on the little things that my game began to show visible improvement. I learned to focus on achieving measurable results rather than how much time I was devoting or how much energy I was expending, and, in the process, I developed self-sustaining routines to propel me forward.

The experience gave me a 180-degree attitude adjustment and new habits I could apply to everything else I did. I didn't work less hard, but I was working much smarter.

It's worth noting again that other people play a role in our success, as discussed in chapter 4. As I said then, we aren't in this alone. Seek out others, directly or indirectly. Find out what worked for them and see if it can work for you. Discover the clues they've left behind. To improve in golf, I hired a golf pro; to get the most out of my workouts, I work with a personal trainer. To design the architecture of my diet, I read a book to guide me. For nearly anything we hope to accomplish, there's someone out there who's done it. Seek them out and learn from their success and failures. We don't need to reinvent the wheel.

Also, always remember that it's the quality of the effort that makes the difference and brings us to our goals. Whatever our long-term game plan, no matter what adjustments we make along the way, we should value the quality of the process more than anything else. When we work smarter, we don't work to get by; we work to learn and evolve. Life is not a check-the-box existence.

Execute each part of your plan with enthusiasm and allegiance to its tiniest details. Elevate your performance to a personal art form. Find joy in the tiny wins and develop habits to last a lifetime. Be smart about each step along the way, minimize the times you stray from the path, and reap the inherent success of your personal journey toward great results.

Have faith in yourself.

Trust the process.

Execute.

6

Emotional Quotient

*"In a very real sense, we have two minds,
one that thinks and one that feels."*

—DANIEL GOLEMAN

In this book, I set out to motivate you to achieve your personal goals and change behaviors in positive ways that last. Among other things, I've talked about finding our individual gifts, identifying a set of core values, engaging in a process of hustle and grind, and bringing a single-minded focus to all that we do.

But there's one essential quality that goes beyond a focus on the individual and into the realm of the social. It concerns how we relate to others in everything we experience, and how interpersonal dynamics can contribute to our own growth and define how we show up each day and, in the end, what we ultimately contribute to the larger community.

Much has been written about emotional intelligence and emotional quotient; take a Google journey and you'll find a depth of knowledge and analysis on both. I don't intend to repeat or even summarize that body of work—far be it from me to claim expertise in that psychological realm. Instead, I'll focus on the role that the emotional quotient plays in the pursuit of life goals within the framework of this book.

Definitions of emotional intelligence can vary. To me, they all come down to self-awareness and self-honesty and our capacity (and willingness) to sensitize to the feelings of others without judgment. The emotional quotient (EQ) is the degree to which our emotional intelligence—some would say maturity—has evolved, or, to put it more colloquially, our capacity to stand in other people's shoes and see and appreciate the world from their emotional eyes.

Recasting the Daniel Goleman quote at the beginning of this chapter, EQ and IQ occupy different sides of the same coin. When operating in tandem, they give us a complete perspective of the emotional drumbeat of the everyday world. It's one thing to be book smart, to accumulate and apply information and develop professional or technical skills. It's quite another to package that expertise and know-how with the ability to connect with people and tune in to their personal and emotional soft spots.

Intellectual brilliance and well-developed expertise in the real world aren't enough. To make sound decisions and chart an effective course toward fulfilling our potential, we need the capacity to positively process emotional responses.

To be clear, I much admire the brilliant mind and skilled practitioner in all walks of life. What brings the greatest and most sustainable rewards, however, is using EQ to drive and mold that talent in the most effective way and leave a legacy of positive impact.

For that reason, I believe EQ is the X factor. It completes us.

People with high EQ tend to get things done because of how they deal with themselves and engage with others. They listen well. They show compassion. They have the courage to see themselves with a broad and deep lens and allow others into their lives to influence them in ways many have never imagined. Their transparency and willingness to adapt open them to sustained and continuous growth.

We all have a well of emotional intelligence to draw on in order to meet emotional challenges each day. Still, it's not something that comes naturally for everyone. In fact, many of us find it challenging, but that doesn't mean we can't nurture and develop it. Using a coach or other professional to help increase EQ is an option, but we also have self-help. We can always look inward to become more aware of who we are and what motivates us and, in the process, develop an evolved sense of what others feel. It often comes down to how much we want to grow, and how honest with ourselves we want to be.

When we stare into our souls for a close look at what we feel and why, we may not always like what we see. We may not like parts of who we are. But that's where courage comes in. That's where, in terms of our commitment to ourselves and others, the rubber meets the road. How badly do we want to change? How willing are we to move outside our comfort zones? This is no different than changing life habits, as discussed earlier. It comes down to willingness. Vigilantly coming to terms with ourselves so we can better appreciate and identify with others is a deeper layer of the hustle and grind process.

I'm the first to admit that none of this is easy. Finding the capacity to see the world through the eyes of others, especially in stressful situations where it often matters most, can sometimes seem insurmountable. Looking deeply into our personal mirror and identifying ways and suitable times to express feelings—including empathy—and affirm others, especially in the workplace, is no less of a challenge.

Doctors, for example, are trained to bring emotional detachment to their work, to keep distance between them and the patient in order to avoid making errors in judgment or losing focus on essential details. But the work of most doctors arises in the human context. Patients don't shelve their emotions when seeking medical attention. On the contrary, patients commonly bring a wealth of anxiety to the doctor's office, even with routine visits, and surgery or a serious diagnosis can trigger a more consuming range of emotions, including fear.

It's not that doctors don't sense or feel what patients are experiencing. It's not that we shut down in the face of obvious patient stress—we respond emotionally just as much as the next person. It's just a matter of how we deal with what we and our patients feel.

As a doctor, I believe it essential to connect with patients in a way that extends genuine empathy. Patients want to feel a connection—they don't want to feel like a widget on an assembly line, passing through the doctor's office like a packaged product. For sure, doctors always need to retain our professional focus and our ability to diagnose and treat without emotional distractions. Showing empathy, however, and real concern for what the patient is experiencing emotionally and physically, can live alongside the professional detachment needed to perform with requisite skill.

This is one reason I don't wear a white coat when seeing patients. To me, the professional garb creates an emotional barrier between the patient and me. I also don't hold a chart in my hand or sit at a computer. I like to sit next to my patient and look at them in the eye. I like to learn about them: what they do for a living, what they did over the weekend, how they spent their holiday, and so on. Creating a bond helps me deliver the best doctoring I can.

It's true that stoicism may be effective and appropriate in various circumstances. Sometimes we must be emotionally detached, especially when delivering bad news. But again, the ability to be clear and firm about medical information doesn't mean we shouldn't show that we care and understand what our patients face or feel in the moment. Our ability to treat patients in this expansive way requires genuine compassion and a sincere effort to know the whole patient, much like we know the loved ones in our life. Patients, like everyone else, matter to their family and friends. They should matter to us as doctors just like our loved ones matter to us. Of course, the degree of tenderness isn't and shouldn't be the same, but the connections are real nonetheless, as is the showing of compassion in both settings.

The ability to be empathetic in the doctor–patient environment is the most beautiful part of being a doctor. It's where we learn about our patients and ourselves.

This all applies to the world outside my professional work. I talked earlier about core values, listing care and compassion as one of my four. At the heart of this value is empathy, and I believe this quality connects us more than any other. We can all feel the emotional triggers of others. We know when others are having a bad day or feeling frustrated or fearful. But how often do we try to lift them up or affirm them in a way that makes them feel better about their day or who they are? How often do we show them the respect that comes with accepting who they are on their terms? What are our instincts in these settings? What do we think we owe others in these moments?

I appreciate that shutting down emotionally when dealing with others can be an effective coping mechanism, much like it often is for doctors. It's certainly easier for a doctor to keep their distance and not have to confront the whirlwind of emotion that may overcome them if they were to try to connect emotionally with patients. The same is true in all other contexts. But we can't hide from the reality that we are emotional creatures as much as we are cognitive creatures, if not more so. We owe it to ourselves and others to recognize and tap into that part of us. It can be tough, but deep within that challenge lies a source of personal power that comes with taking brave steps in building functional relationships that honor others and ourselves.

The late Maya Angelou said, "I've learned that people will forget what you said, people will forget what you did, but people will never forget how you made them feel."

In short, it comes down to this: we're all much better off being kind. A popular bumper sticker exhorts us to "practice random acts of kindness." Some of us may belittle or make jokes about that sticker, but in my view, Anne Herbert, who I understand came up with that slogan in 1982, was onto something profound.

For as long as I can remember, I've always loved the satisfaction I've felt when lending someone a helping hand. I also learned at a young age the profound, unanticipated positive karmic impact good deeds yield.

When we moved to Long Island, there was an elderly couple who lived on our block, Vito and Edna Colliani. Mr. Vito, as I called him, was the de facto mayor of our block. He knew the ins and outs of each house and kept a watchful eye on the neighborhood. His son, who was often deployed abroad for extended periods, would leave his dog Annie with Mr. Vito and Ms. Colliani while away. Because I loved dogs, I'd often join Mr. Vito and Annie on their walks.

When I was about nine, Mr. Vito and his wife planned to leave town for a week and asked if I'd watch Annie while they were away. My responsibilities were to walk her four times a day and handle the feeding chores. I jumped at the chance—I loved that dog—and dutifully took care of her.

When they returned, the Collianis kindly gave me an envelope filled with cash to thank me for a job well done. I had never had a tooth fairy visit or an allowance and so the cash was tempting. Still, I refused to accept the money. My reward was the joy of taking care of the dog. The Collianis, however, wouldn't take no for an answer and sent me on my way with the envelope. When my mom caught wind of it, she wasn't happy. She insisted I return the money. That put me in a bind. I knew Mr. Vito wouldn't go along. So, that night, I tried to sneak the envelope under the Collianis' door, only to get caught, red-handed, in the act.

I explained my predicament to Mr. Vito, and he agreed to take the envelope back on the condition I join him and his wife for supper one night. I, of course, agreed.

That dinner remains one of my fondest childhood memories. The three of us enjoyed a delicious home cooked Italian dinner and hung out afterwards. Their gratitude and kindness gave me a beautiful and enduring memory, something infinitely more valuable than a cash filled envelope. Mr. Vito unfortunately passed away many years ago, but his wife Edna is vital as ever, now well into her 90s. I was blessed to have her celebrate our wedding and, to this day, she sends me notes whenever she spots me in the print press or on television.

Whether it was walking an elderly neighbor's dog as a young boy or helping the new kid in school get acclimated, something felt right when giving. Although I couldn't articulate it as a boy, looking back, I think it was the feeling of injecting good karma into the world I loved. I know it sounds a little hokey, but I do think there is real value in old phrases like "what goes around comes around" or "you reap what you sow." Of course, these phrases generally refer to the negative consequences of actions, but I'm a big believer in the converse being equally true.

People don't turn off their emotional spigots just because they go to work or enter another more formal setting. Depending on the context, they may control their emotions even more, but they still are who they are, which manifests in virtually every circumstance in some manner. As the saying goes, "wherever you go, there you are."

I also value the karmic power of what we leave behind in our emotional dealings. I subscribe to the notion that what goes around comes around. Much like success leaves clues, so does our behavior, especially in dealing with others. We each leave our emotional mark in everything we do, as Maya Angelou pointed out so well. What better way than invoking the power of positivity and not the drag of negativity.

Loving what you do and who you are, exuding positivity, and being kind to others in all its splendor, are what good karma is all about. I firmly believe that the world changes for the better through tiny wins each time we put out positive vibes.

The way we interact in our personal sphere is a microcosm of how we interact with the world. It applies in all contexts—the community we have in the workplace is analogous to the relationship we have with the outside world. Are you the type of person who's going to hold the door open for someone walking into a coffee shop? Are you going to help someone carry their groceries if they could use the help? Conversely, do you have tunnel vision and see only your wants and needs? Are you so self-absorbed in the complexity of your life that you unwittingly ignore others, or worse, run roughshod over them?

It's important to have a we-based mindset, whether in the workplace, at home, or while making our way through the world amid strangers. The energy we put out is the energy we get back, rewarding us tenfold. We're all connected.

Here's an example.

I saw a patient not long ago who also happened to be a medical student. She was on a specific medication for a skin condition, which, because of changes in her insurance coverage, cost her a relative fortune. She also had the burden of paying for blood work and covering the co-pay for her many anticipated office visits. All this put her between a financial rock and a hard place, and one day she opened up to me about the money hardship. She said she wanted to continue her treatment but didn't think she could afford it. I could see she was stressed.

I couldn't do anything about the prohibitive cost of the medication, but a partial solution was for her to have her blood work done at her medical school, which wouldn't charge her. But in addition to the cost of the medication, she had the cost of the co-pays for office visits, which with the anticipated multiple visits, promised to balloon to a hefty number for her.

So, I made her this offer. I said, "Don't pay me anything, but promise that when you become a doctor, someday you'll do for a patient what we're doing for you."

She was on the verge of tears as she asked, "Are you serious?"

I told her I was.

For me, it was a golden opportunity to inject a small dose of good karma into the world. Her heartfelt reaction underscored the good feeling I had about the whole thing.

Little things make a difference. For me, the karmic impact of the gesture held significantly more value than the income from the aggregate co-pays. The reward was knowing that I'd infused good energy into the universe and that she would someday replicate what we did for her, creating a positive vibe that I know will someday make its way back to me in some form. Paying it forward is what it's all about.

It's not only the art of our skilled performance that matters, but also the personal impact we leave behind. Whatever good karma you put out there, you'll be rewarded. Trust me. So, let's do it. Let's create good karma. Let's sprinkle the world with positive encrgy.

7

The Reward of Criticism

"Do not seek praise. Seek criticism."
—PAUL ARDEN

Earlier we explored the value of mentors and other influencers in our lives, and how we aren't alone in the never-ending quest for growth and goal achievement. Opportunities to fuel change with the help of others surround us, strengthening our ability to enjoy success in whatever we do and whoever we want to become.

The same can be said of criticism.

To most, the word "criticism" is associated with the family of negatives, like finding fault with someone's performance or conduct or receiving less than flattering comments or a put-down. It can also, however, refer to a thoughtful opinion or a piece of constructive feedback.

It's important to distinguish criticism from judgment. Criticism can be positive; judgment is almost always negative. I like to look at criticism as a rich source of valuable information—morsels of data to process, evaluate and use productively. Judgment, on the other hand, is often fueled by negativity, resentment, and jealousy. Judgment provides little or no value, and, if allowed to infiltrate your mindset, can stifle growth and progress and produce a domino effect of frustration and negativity.

In a general sense, however, I think it's fair to say that most of us don't jump for joy when we receive criticism. Nor do we go out of our way to find it. Naturally, we want to be liked and valued, and criticism can often feel like a blow to those desires, whether intended or not. It can hurt.

Criticism can also prompt a wide range of natural human reactions. We can minimize or downplay the gist of what we're hearing, come up with seat-of-the-pants excuses or semantical quibbles to parry the onslaught of words, or retreat and set up barricades. Sometimes, when temperatures rise, we point fingers to flip the narrative or even lash out. If allowed, criticism can be combustible.

I've come to see criticism and feedback as an interplay between self-perception and self-awareness, where our emotional quotient (EQ), discussed in the previous chapter, plays an important role. At its core, criticism is a way to communicate and relate to each other. How we handle and process criticism is a window into who we are—or can be—and how well we interact with others.

When someone lobs critical comments our way, whether tongue in cheek, to offer earnest feedback, or out of frustration or anger, the first thing most of us instinctively do is channel what we're hearing through the image we have of ourselves. Does it affirm who we think we are or cast shade on our self-perception? If the information we're receiving doesn't square with how we see ourselves in the world, our knee-jerk reaction is often to recoil from what's being said.

Sometimes we're so ill-disposed to hear the criticism that we don't even wait until the speaker is finished before we launch into our self-defense. Think about a time you injected a rousing defense while someone was in mid-sentence with comments you perceived as negative and unhelpful, or something you simply didn't want to hear.

As suggested, helpful feedback doesn't always imply negative behavior or that we've crossed a line or done something wrong. It may be something else entirely. It can be subtle, or it may only concern us indirectly but nonetheless be crucial for us to hear.

Here's a personal example. I see myself as a polite, relaxed, and accessible person. I like to think I project a sense of caring for others, that I'm empathetic and a good listener. I rarely get upset and assume that people feel like they can easily approach me. With this self-image, it's understandable that when my wife told me that others find me intimidating before they get to know me, I was taken aback.

When she told me this, I was incredulous. "Me? The chill me? Intimidating? Ha. No way!" She was describing someone I didn't recognize at first; she was offering an image that didn't fit with the persona I thought I'd constructed for myself. It was as if she was trying to fit a square peg into a round hole.

But I took it to heart. I didn't feel less myself; I didn't feel like my self-image was a form of self-deception. I focused on understanding how the image I had of myself might be misconstrued or filtered through a lens that dramatically altered the impact of what I intended. This allowed me to be more in tune with others and how I make them feel, even if what they feel isn't what I intend. It made me realize that it's not only how I see myself that matters in interactions, but also how others see themselves in a scenario, which includes how I come off to them, however well intentioned I am.

It was valuable feedback and another powerful lesson in the realm of emotional intelligence. It wasn't too long after this that it also played out in the office.

I share a great relationship with an employee who, after working with me for over a year, said to me, "God, you're such a pushover. I can't believe I was scared of you in the beginning, you know?"

My internal reaction was, "Really? You're kidding me. You were afraid of me?"

Her candor flashed me back to the discussion with my wife. I knew that what my employee perceived at the beginning of her employment had much to do with our different professional and office roles, but her comment still made me think long and hard about what I might have done or said, or what I'd projected, to trigger that initial reaction in her. It forced me again to examine how I could adjust my demeanor, tone, and body language to help others feel more comfortable, trustful, and encouraged.

I want to bring people in, not push them away, and if I wanted genuine feedback, I had to do a better job of nurturing an environment in which others were comfortable sharing criticism and honest thoughts.

I had to know others' perception of me to better know myself.

When it comes to interpersonal dynamics and the value of feedback, it's important to keep in mind that the message isn't always about us. Often, it's about how others "process" us, or what our demeanor or style conjures up within them. Oscar Wilde said, "Criticism is the only reliable form of autobiography." While perhaps a silver-tongued overstatement, it holds much truth, underscoring how criticism is often more about the speaker than the intended recipient.

Still, even when this is the case, there's value in what we hear. It uncovers how we fit into the perceptions of others and fill out their experiences. It teaches us to stay mindful of the undercurrents and less obvious dynamics in scenarios. Stubbornly refusing to pay attention to the cues in our interactions can free our ego to trample over our ability to connect well with others. We must know and respect our audience. If we want to communicate effectively, expand our influence, and enrich our contributions to the world, we must make adjustments that reflect an honest assessment of how we come off to other people.

Criticism is a window into ourselves and others.

It's not uncommon for people to critique or criticize others out of fear or frustration. But these moments also hold value by presenting opportunities to understand others better and develop internal skills that allow us to manage tough moments and become a more evolved person. Don't attack the messenger. Rather, untangle the content from the speaker by stepping back, taking control, and finding the value.

For sure, not everyone is skilled at providing feedback or criticism and the value of their words can easily be lost in their delivery. We can't control how others transmit information to us, but we can control our ability to find value in what's said, no matter how poorly it's conveyed. Hiding inside frustration because of how someone speaks to us, while often understandable, doesn't advance the ball. We can and should be better than that. We owe it to ourselves to find a way to rise above the clouded part of the message.

Even if we don't react well in the moment, once the dust settles, we can find the gift in what happened. Think about how many times someone has gone postal on you and gotten your blood boiling. After you'd calmed down, you were probably able to realize that their tantrum had nothing to do with you, but rather with some other outside stressor—you were just their punching bag. Once we're clear on the reality of what happened, we can derive substantial benefit from the experience: what we heard, what we said, how we said it, and how we reacted. We don't always need to have it together when the storm hits, so long as we right the ship after things settle down.

Next we come to the most common form of criticism: commentary designed to evaluate skills, performance, or behavior. Examples of this include employment reviews, academic paper evaluations, or fitness assessments. When these critiques don't align with our self-perception, our reactions can be much the same as in personal situations. The criticism can provoke fear or make us feel bad about what we've done or not done well enough. Hearing that we've fallen short in performance, or that we aren't getting the job done as well as we thought, or in keeping with someone's expectations, can be difficult to digest.

The bottom line is that there is no escaping criticism. It's unavoidable and must be taken head-on and handled one way or another. If we're living an engaging life, testing ourselves and getting outside our comfort zone, pushing personal envelopes, and blazing our trails with passion, we'll encounter an abundance of criticism. It comes with the territory whenever we're engaged in the hustle and grind.

In the words of Aristotle, "There is only one way to avoid criticism: do nothing, say nothing, and be nothing."

Everyone has an opinion, their two cents to offer, and most of the time they're inclined to offer it whether we've asked for it or not. The question is, who's speaking? What are their qualifications? What's their experience or background? Where are they coming from? Objectively, why should you value what they have to say?

For example, as discussed earlier, I got a lot of pushback when I first jumped into social media with my Instagram posts and podcasts. Those with the loudest negative voices either didn't understand or appreciate social media or were simply hating on or judging me (and remember, judgment is virtually valueless). It was foreign to them, and, as far as they were concerned, too far outside the box of how a dermatologist should behave. Because those viewpoints were neither informed nor aligned with my goals, I paid them no mind. Instead, I listened to those who understood the potential of social media and knew a thing or two about how to make it work. I sought their advice and absorbed *their* feedback.

In other words, I considered the sources of the criticism and set appropriate boundaries.

When the matter is more personal, it becomes more complex. How well does the person know you? How well do they understand human behavior? Do they have an agenda? Is it about them and not you?

For example, when my wife comments on something I've done or said, I pay attention, not only for the sake of my relationship, but also because no one knows me better than she does. The same is true in the workplace. Some of my employees know me better, or at least in a different way, than many of my friends. When they're speaking on matters they know, their feedback has value and I cherish the opportunity to hear from them.

Our ability to use criticism to our advantage is a life skill. It's where the growth mindset popularized by Carol

Dweck in *Mindset: The New Psychology of Success* comes in handy. Her book underscores using feedback as a vital source for learning rather than swatting it away like a pesky fly or viewing it as a negative force.

Go the extra mile by engaging the criticizer in an inquisitive manner. Dissect their message and drill down on what they mean. Affirm statements you agree with and try to understand statements that confuse you or throw you off. Get examples and harvest their wisdom. A dialogue without judgment, where you're open to the possibilities, will only generate positive results. You can always accept what you like and let the rest go, but you won't experience the full breadth of the available benefits without an open dialogue.

When we receive and absorb pearls of wisdom, we expand our horizons. We learn to listen better. We become better problem solvers. We become humbler and more patient, widening our apertures for personal growth. Our relationships improve. Our EQ rises.

Harvesting criticism empowers us. It effects real change, sometimes in small incremental steps, much like the tiny wins we enjoy when we change our habits. It's another opportunity to grab the wheel and get in control of our destiny.

As we manage criticism, we develop new positive habits that are no less important—and arguably more import-ant—than the others we've explored. As we develop strong habits in managing criticism, we increase the ability to exhibit grace in our responses. How many times have you offered sharp feedback to someone and were met with open arms in response? This doesn't happen often, but when it does, it disarms the speaker and softens the circumstances, inspiring honesty, heightening self-awareness, and forging meaningful connections.

For me, the end game, the breakthrough, is craving criticism by making it integral to how we view ourselves and conduct our lives, and seeing it as an essential ingredient of our path to success. In this way, we transform criticism from something to tolerate into an ally and powerful tool. Don't wait for criticism to arrive. Seek it from those whose perspective you trust and whose experience, wisdom, and candor you value. It will deepen and expand your potential and cultivate your success.

8

Fail Your Way to Success

"Once you know what failure feels like,
determination chases success."

—KOBE BRYANT

The mere mention of failure can cause our heart to skip a beat and conjure up negative thoughts that threaten doom. Avoid failure like the plague, that inner voice says.

What if it was precisely the opposite? What if you welcomed or even yearn for failure? What if it wasn't a defeat, but an asset? What if failure was uniquely valuable? How would your life be different if you viewed failure as a gift?

Failure is cut from the same cloth as criticism—both are inevitable throughout our lives; both can cut painfully deep, throw us off-balance, and feel like a staggering blow.

They can also both be difference makers, give us choices, and, if we're good students of ourselves, teach us.

Failure and criticism have an important difference in that the impact of failure can be more far-reaching than criticism. Failure can present life-altering challenges and redefine how we approach the world and see ourselves more than criticism tends to.

On the one hand, failure can stop us dead in our tracks and send us into a spiral of self-defeat, zapping our spirit. On the other, it can inspire reflection, provide important new information, help us reshape our vision, and, to borrow from the late Kobe Bryant, give us renewed determination. The contrast between the two scenarios is deep and bright, and it leads to dramatically different places.

What if we viewed failure in an even more radical way, as more than an event that provides choices but a *requirement* to success?

In this light, failure serves as a benchmark for commitment, demonstrating how much we truly want to be engaged in what we're doing. It personifies the boldness of risk-taking and pushing the envelope in the quest for fulfillment. It's what lies at the epicenter of the hustle and grind. The harder your drive, the more you'll fail, and the more you fail, the more often and the greater you'll succeed.

Failure is like a wall that unavoidably springs up in the middle of the road we've chosen for our life journeys. There it sits, blocking our way, defiantly daring us to take it on. What should we do? Feel sorry for ourselves? Become immobilized? Bow our heads and drag ourselves home?

Or, do we reassess and explore ways to conquer that wall? Go through it? Circumvent it? Climb over it?

Appreciate that the wall representing failure isn't a roadblock; it's a place for a temporary stop and maybe a detour. Rather than representing the end of the journey, it's the beginning of a new one. Failure either controls us or we find a way to make it work for us.

Medical school brought me face-to-face with failure that easily could've jeopardized my professional goals and spun me toward directions unknown. As I mentioned earlier, I'd acquired some poor academic habits in high school, but I still managed to graduate in the top 10 percent of my class and get a decent score on the SAT. Even in college, applying myself minimally, I was able to graduate with close to a 4.0 GPA. I tended to wing it and game the system, doing the absolute minimum amount of work required to score an A, which, quite honestly, was my only goal. Again, I presumed I could get by because I had an exceptional memory. And get by I did. I presumed that everything was fine.

It all came to a head in a histology class, a highly focused course that delves into the intricacies and functions of tissues, cells, and organs. For most medical students, histology was a requisite, garden-variety class to check off the list to get a medical degree. For them, knowing the basics was good enough. For me, however, histology was an essential foundational class—I wanted to practice both dermatology and pathology, which meant that, in addition to treating clinical patients, I would spend many an hour looking at tissue and cells under a microscope to diagnose various skin conditions. Histology, in other words, was on the short list of classes I had to master.

You may think I would've been all in for this class. You'd be wrong. I rarely, if ever, attended the lectures and I skipped nearly every lab session, missing out on workshops where the class examined and studied slides—an activity that was to become a critical part of my medical career. Don't get me wrong; I didn't ignore the content entirely. I set out to cram the material in my usual way, this time by watching videos (instead of attending class), which was a CliffsNotes-esque shortcut. I assumed that when all was said and done, armed with my typical strategy and methods, I could put in minimal effort and still get a good grade. After all, that was my way, winging it. It had worked for me an infinite number of times before. Why not again?

Well, as it turned out, I didn't merely score poorly—I got a whopping F.

I now faced a situation that threatened to become a slippery slope and imperil my dream of becoming a dermatologist, which was the hardest field to match into and get offered residencies (post-graduate training prerequisite to getting a medical license) and fellowships (training in a medical specialty). I had a choice: I could continue my errant ways and endanger my career even more, or I could find a way around the wall I'd managed to construct and learn a valuable lesson in the process.

The F in histology wasn't my first wake-up call in medical school; by this time, my friend Sami Khan had already given me a proverbial kick in the pants. Evidently, I hadn't sufficiently heeded the wisdom of his advice. It was déjà vu.

This time, the F grade gave me a major jolt and taught

me a lesson about myself in time to make amends. It was a come-to-Jesus moment. I told myself, "you have to be done with shortcuts. You have to stop that nonsense." I knew I could no longer tolerate that sort of behavior in myself if I had serious intentions of becoming the kind of doctor I knew I could be and was expected to become. I took a long look in the mirror and acknowledged that I had a natural tendency to slip into "lazy mode." I had to understand, without making excuses, that if left unchecked, that trait could undermine everything I wanted to achieve. I needed to overcome the tendency to wing it. I could no longer take things in my professional life for granted. This had to be the last time.

I went to my histology teacher, hat in hand, and gave a heartfelt mea culpa. He was understanding and, more importantly, generous enough to give me a chance at redemption. He allowed me to take the class again during the summer—a life raft I grabbed without hesitancy. I got an A the second time around.

This experience taught me that failing isn't about losing; it's about discovering. I'd uncovered a flaw in myself that I needed to isolate and manage at a deeper level. Failure had become an asset.

I took my lesson in stride. I didn't rejoice. I didn't jump for joy. I simply moved on, humbled and maybe wiser. I had no desire to publicize my stumble, and I buried the incident and didn't talk about it. That seemed natural then, but I wondered later, why not celebrate failure? How rare is it for someone to say, "I'm thrilled that I failed" or "I'm proud I failed?" or "I'm glad I failed, because by failing I learned and grew."

Everyone, at one time or another, has overlooked the beauty of the positive aspects of failure. We allow the experience to cast a long shadow instead of discovering and exploiting the gifts in the setback—the teachings that can transform us. How different the world would be if we exalted our failures as powerful teaching tools. Those experiences are more than silver linings in a dark cloud; they're the core parts we find in ourselves to build upon and grow. Failure can teach us what we didn't know we needed to succeed.

Success exists within failure in the form of a seed of new success that can then be planted. The failures of the most successful people—where they stumbled and got up, and how they used their failures to propel them to great heights—are well chronicled.

For example, Michael Jordan, considered one of the best basketball players of all time, got cut from his high school basketball team. The rest is legend. Thomas Edison made one thousand failed attempts before he figured out how to design a working light bulb. Bill Gates's first company lost so much money that it tanked—he used the lessons of that failure to launch Microsoft. Oprah Winfrey conquered an unimaginable upbringing and a disheartening demotion before launching her hugely successful media career. The list goes on.

What distinguishes successful people is their ability to both overcome the emotional deflation of failure and life challenges and use their experiences as launching pads to reach new heights and get them where they want to go. They're powerful models of the hustle and grind.

What about taking it to yet another level and viewing failure as a goal we plot for ourselves?

For example, my physical trainer once urged me to add jumping rope to my workout regime. I pushed back, telling him I didn't know how to jump rope. End of discussion, right? Except he kept insisting that I should give it a try— after all, *everyone* knows how to jump rope, he told me. Left with little choice, I obliged, and, as I expected and feared, I failed instantly and demonstrably (in front of a packed gym, mind you!). My heart started racing. The other trainers came over, forming a circle around me, giving me pointers and cheering me on. I tried again, and, no surprise, failed again. It was a spectacle. Everyone in the gym could see that this thirty-six-year-old wannabe-stud could not jump rope. I was center stage and I was hugely embarrassed—my ego took a direct hit. I was athletic, but that instant failure taught me that jumping rope required more athleticism than I had. Like riding a bike, it required a specific type of coordination and skill, and it was painfully obvious that I didn't have either.

Once the embarrassment passed, I went inside myself for a discussion with my internal voices. The loudest and most persuasive argued that I'd come too far in my training to start playing small. I knew I had to practice what I preached about comfort zones. I knew I had to come to grips with my ego and fear of failure and make them work for me.

When I got home, I ordered a jump rope from Amazon. Two days later, shiny new jump rope in hand, I began to watch video after video on YouTube, getting schooled in the art of jumping rope. Each day, for thirty minutes to an hour, I buried myself in those videos. I practiced each day, wherever mirrors were in my home, with no self-consciousness. I stumbled and struggled and kept on—my wife and children thought some screws had come loose. But one day, I was able to show my trainer that I had it down.

My jump rope skills were so abysmal from the get-go that even my trainer was taken aback at my newfound skill. Learning to jump rope may seem like a silly and trivial hurdle, but it taught me another profound lesson about failure. The wall of failure is more than something to overcome; it's a requirement, a necessary stepping-stone, to get to the next level. To this day, nearly eight years later, my trainer and I often refer to this story as an example of what defines a success-based mindset, namely embracing and owning failure and working relentlessly to push past it. This mindset is essential for success in the gym, in the workplace, and in life.

Part of the value of accepting the interconnectedness of success and failure is that success has its limitations as a teacher, while failure teaches resilience and often brings helpful new information. It's hard to succeed without resilience, and without acquiring a steady flow of know-how to refine and adapt your direction. Of course, it may not be easy to equate failing with learning. Failure can bruise the ego, sometimes badly, and bring personal embarrassment, as in my jumping rope experience, and in the process can damage or topple self-confidence. Converting failure into a positive requires courage and a get-after-it attitude.

Embracing failure not only prepares us for what comes next, but also dilutes our fears about stumbling, feeling ashamed, or being judged. When we don't fear failure, when it's welcomed and even sought after, we become empowered to innovate more, take more risk, and test more boundaries. It can be a major personal breakthrough.

Quieting our fear of failure also helps us deal with the attachments that clog our brains and block our vision. For example, it's natural and common to become wedded to an image we have of ourselves, of how we envision ourselves in the world. When disappointing circumstances arise that don't feed that image, we can get angry, frustrated, or confused, or worse, we can blame others for our perceived shortcomings.

The feeling of going nowhere fast in the face of failure can also happen when we find ourselves glued to expectations we project to the point that they become a "make it or break it" or "my way or the highway" situation. Again, like what can happen when we fixate on a self-image, when these expectations don't pan out, we can easily find ourselves overwhelmed with disappointment, thus derailing our plans.

When it comes to leveraging failure toward positive outcomes, these internal attachments can be severely limiting, sometimes even becoming an albatross (a psychological burden that feels like a curse). This slide backward, however, is avoidable by looking in the mirror and putting self-awareness and self-honesty at a premium.

This harkens to the discussion about mindset and comfort zones. Having a healthy relationship with failure in the big picture and not sweating the small stuff in the everyday world makes it exponentially easier to change how we see and experience setbacks. Imagine being grateful for failure. Imagine failure as a trusted ally.

The simplest approach for dealing with failure is to mine the experience for nuggets of new information and knowledge. If you focus on doing this, overcoming the failure and turning it into an asset will come more easily. What did you learn? What strengths did it reveal? What limitations or weaknesses did it expose? What did the failure tell you about yourself, and how did that match up with your existing self-image? What strategic lessons did it teach you, and how do these potentially impact your next steps?

The Apollo 13 mission popularized the phrase "failure is not an option." In the life-or-death situation those astronauts faced, those five words became a powerful rallying cry. But in the world where most of us live, failure is a real option, and much more than that: it's essential. Perhaps our mantra should be that "*accepting* failure is not an option."

Failing provides an affirmation that we are, in fact, on the right path.

The spirit of the hustle and grind invites failure through full-on engagement. What often separates successful people is their mindset about this. Being "all in" only becomes true if we take risks and relish the failures that teach us and propel us forward.

Be bold. Make failure a contributing part of your path to success.

9

The Architecture of Diet

"The groundwork of all happiness is health."

—LEIGH HUNT

It's a moment that remains emblazoned on my memory, and it happened in a setting that couldn't have been scripted better.

In 2012, my family had assembled for Thanksgiving, indulging in the food bounty as families do on that occasion, catching up and enjoying each other's company. When the meal was almost over and that too-much-to-eat, bulging discomfort had begun to take over, my brother-in-law, a year younger than I, leaned back, turned to me, and said, "Dude, what the hell happened to us?" Except he didn't use the word "hell," and he didn't have to explain what he meant.

His tone was partly in jest, but at the core, he was dead serious, even a little sad. He was referring to the sorry condition of our bodies.

At the time, we were both under forty and had bellies. We'd gotten dough-boy soft. It wasn't as if I had no clue, but his comment triggered an onslaught of feelings. I felt ashamed, and I suffered the expected bruising of the ego.

His comment ended up sparking a life-changing epiphany.

I'd developed the dreaded "dad bod," a sorry condition that afflicts many fathers who lose their way physically when their life takes the dramatic and exhilarating turn after they have children. Being a new parent radically changes virtually every aspect of your life, and having more than one child complicates things exponentially. As I quickly learned, your life becomes all about the kids—what was previously a focus on my wife, job, and myself became a focus on the enjoyment and well-being of my children. I downgraded my needs in favor of life on the home front.

While they bring boundless joy, children are exhausting; for parents, food can become a response, something to squeeze in when you can to help ease the pressure. Eat when and what you can, as fast as you can. There's too much else to do.

For me, each successive child brought more slothfulness, bad habits, and inattention to my physical condition. My priorities changed, and as they did, the rolls on my body grew, amassing ounce by ounce, pound by pound over time. It was barely noticeable at first and then one day, I took a good look and didn't like what I saw.

To be honest, I was never an Adonis. Since my teenage years, I was the prototypical "skinny-fat"—I managed to look lean, but I was a flabby mess. By the time my brother-in-law made his well-timed call to arms during that fateful Thanksgiving meal, however, I had either lost self-awareness or stopped caring. I had let myself go. I was in a terrible rut. Even worse, next to my beautiful wife, who somehow effortlessly recovered her slender physique after each pregnancy, I looked like the potbellied Indian uncles of my youth.

When my brother-in-law flashed that glaring light on our sorry physical selves, it triggered a commitment to change. To aid the incentive and inject some fun into the process, he and I made a wager to see who could lose the most pounds and get in better shape by Memorial Day, six months later. A dash of competition can be a useful ingredient.

By Memorial Day, I went from 196 pounds of putty to 154 pounds and 8 percent body fat. I like to think I won the bet, although my brother-in-law claims we tied. He's my wife's little brother, and a good guy, so I'll give him the benefit of the doubt and agree with him. The important point is that we both set out to make major changes in our lives, for our health and our families, and we got it done. It became another game-changing experience.

But my transformation wasn't all about going to the gym and marching to the beat of a personal trainer, although the rigorous workout routine I developed played a critical part. It was a combination of fitness and nutrition that gave me the impetus for real and sustained change in my life. Looking good counts for little if what's happening inside doesn't follow suit.

It's impossible for any substantial body transformation to occur without proper attention to nutrition. During the period of my physical decline, I'm ashamed to say that I had been working, even with a trainer at times. Yet my body got flabbier year after year because my diet was an undisciplined mishmash of bagels, pizza, and beer. I learned the hard way that abs are truly made in the kitchen, not the gym.

If I was sincere about wanting to change my body, I had to change my diet and lifestyle. Keeping my goal of getting "jacked" in mind, my trainer and I developed a three- to five-year conditioning and nutrition plan. Nutrition and exercise go hand in hand. It was my version of Sanjay Gupta meets The Rock.

We each have favorite foods we can't seem to do without, and lifestyles vary widely. I don't expect others to copy what I did, but I do think we each need to step back and figure out a nutrition and diet regime that serves us well. It doesn't need to be the same as anyone else's, but it needs to be carefully considered and designed to work in the unique context of your life.

I realize that putting a nutrition plan together isn't automatic; you can't snap your fingers and voilà, have a nutrition plan you're willing to live by. Conferring with a nutritionist or exploring other valuable resources is helpful and may even be necessary to devise the right approach. But regardless of how your plan is devised, appreciate that the dividends are too significant to pass up and, once again, it's in your hands.

I call my program the "architecture of diet." I've been on this path for several years, and it's produced countless benefits for me. I'm healthier and stronger and I have considerably more energy. Because of the changes I made after that fateful Thanksgiving years ago, I move through each day with an extra bounce in my step. I feel empowered.

Before getting into the details, I'd like to point out what many don't want to hear when it comes to this topic: being compliant with a studious nutrition program often means a diet that tends to be less than awe-inspiring. My wife is fond of chiding me for the lack of inspiration, diversity, and style in my diet. In a word, she calls it boring. I can't argue with that—my diet is boring. But I've found that consistency is key, just like working out at the gym. You can't come at this half-assed. Most days I eat the exact same thing. I've transformed what food means to me in my life. It generally isn't something I crave; it's what I use for fuel.

The foundation for my nutritional plan over the last seven-plus years is intermittent fasting, where I consume my calories between 12 PM and 8 PM. Adhering to that schedule has freed me to not think about food, liberating me from the shackles food often clamps on us. I don't give food that much thought anymore. I have a system I follow, and it works wonderfully for me.

I fast in the morning, drinking black coffee without any milk or sugar. I drink water, though I prefer sparkling water because it fills the stomach. I generally break my fast around noon.

The noon hour is when I have breakfast: eggs or sometimes an egg sandwich on a whole wheat roll with soup or something similar. It's enough to keep me going. Then, around two or three o'clock, I'll treat myself to ten ounces of meat with some vegetables and rice. When I'm in my New York City office, I order from one of two restaurants, each time the exact same meal. When I'm in my Long Island office, I do the same. Then, for dinner, it's déjà vu: protein, starch (usually rice), and vegetables (including potatoes).

That sums up my regular diet. Virtually each day. Boring, right?

When I started my nutritional plan, I weighed each portion of what I ate to determine how many macronutrients (protein, carbs, and fat) I was taking in. I know that sounds obsessive and extreme, but I found it to be critical. Measuring what I ate not only allowed me to develop an effective program, but it also taught me about food quantity and composition. I no longer need to weigh my food; now I can eyeball food items on a plate and get a good handle on their macronutrients. Because of my regular routine in the early days, this became an acquired skill and is now an integral part of how I approach diet and nutrition. I might even go so far as to say that one can't manage diet effectively without going through a similar exercise.

The food measuring I did is an apt illustration of attention to detail, which is a core value of mine. Laser-focusing on the details of diet and food isn't fundamentally different than the awareness needed in professions and other activities. For example, in my medical office, my staff members are precise and keenly focused whenever inputting a patient's name, insurance, and other information into their medical record. The same is true when I perform a biopsy or make sure everything is in place for a surgical procedure. The context may be different, but the mindset is identical.

If you're trying to get into shape and you simply say, as I so often hear, "I'm going to eat healthy," you're doomed from the start. A specific, detailed plan is required to get results. Ask yourself: are you attentive to each detail of your diet, including the composition of what you're putting into your body as well as how much and how often you're eating? Are you attentive to your macronutrient requirements, your carbs, protein and fats? Do you know enough about what you eat to avoid pitfalls or risky trends? How much control do you truly have over your diet and personal nutritional program? Conversely, how much do you cede to others or bad, thoughtless habits?

It takes patience and time to build positive momentum and entrench yourself in good habits, regardless of the circumstances. Once you're there, veering off course every now and then doesn't undermine the program. On weekends, if I'm going out to dinner with my wife or meeting friends and I want to have a few drinks or maybe some bites of dessert, it doesn't kill my diet because I enter that particular weekend by design with a caloric deficit. I plan for it. This allows me to consume more calories, which I sometimes do intentionally. As a result, these little cheats don't affect me—they wind up being short-lived, temporary stoppages in the hustle and grind of my vigorous diet. Besides, we all deserve occasional indulgences. They give us balance.

Vacations are an entirely different matter. They can be challenging. Admittedly, on family vacations, my discipline takes its own vacation. I drink more and cheat more with what I eat. But oddly, I always tend to lose weight on vacation, possibly at the risk of losing muscle mass. I've learned not to beat myself up about it. I'm committed and disciplined enough to know that I'll ease into my routine once I'm home.

Dropping off the path by having a temporary lapse in your nutrition regime is like taking a bad turn off the straight path up the mountain and winding up on a series of switchbacks. You'll still get to your destination, but it may take longer and be more difficult en route. You can't beat yourself up about it and you can't let it become the norm.

Veering off the good-habit path and trying to recover isn't always easy; returning to the discipline that serves us so well can be tough. Self-awareness, self-honesty, and a deep sense of commitment are the keys to getting back on track.

The bottom line is that no matter how diligent we are, we will have moments when our eating habits resemble the untamed ways of our high school days. We will sometimes assume the couch potato position and take a hiatus from exercising. These momentary setbacks are expected, but they should be relegated to the once-in-a-while category.

It's daunting to pour yourself into a tightly structured workout and diet regime. The changes in habit and lifestyle can be intimidating. It comes back to the tiny-wins mentality. Can you find satisfaction in a daily nutritional regime? Can you place value on each day, each meal, each bite, each swallow?

This is where attention to detail, good habits, and goal setting converge for the short and long term. It helps to identify what we want to accomplish each day in terms of what and when we eat—every tiny win gets us closer to our goal. Proceeding in this manner, step by step, builds a strong and lasting foundation for good habits.

Focusing only on the long term will never work; it's overwhelming and inhibiting. It's the small, incremental, and well-defined daily steps taken toward the goal that bring success.

I've come to appreciate that diligent exercise and diet regimes are part of a holistic lifestyle adjustment—separately, they don't get the job done. At the end of the day, it all comes down to the hustle and grind mindset.

I'm the first to acknowledge that we can often be mindless about what we eat and drink. As busy people, we often don't pay attention to the details of what we ingest. But what we put into our bodies is as essential to our well-being as what we do with our bodies. It's not only about building a strong and healthy body, it's also about providing fuel for our daily performance in whatever we do. There is no escaping that reality.

I know it's become a cliché, but the truth is, success is

a journey, not a destination. Fitness and nutrition plans are vital components of that journey. Someone doesn't spend years and years getting into shape only to arrive at that goal and then start eating like there's no tomorrow and giving up exercise. You keep pushing the limits and upping your goals. It's a cycle that builds on itself.

Again, my specific approach, how I design the architecture of diet, while a good fit for me, may not resonate with everyone. Whatever the details, find a routine that suits you well, one you can master in order to get to where you want to go and who you want to be. The first few months will reveal whether the plan is working for your body and what adjustments you may need to make. But sticking with it is key. When you start eating a little bit better, you start feeling a little better and exercising a little more. What follows is a rewarding and enduring cycle of positivity.

To this day, I'm still shocked when people refer to me as an in-shape or muscular guy. It's funny, because when I look in the mirror, I see the skinny-fat flabby guy hiding behind this new physique I've worked so hard to obtain. That said, as hard as it is to recognize change in myself, it's indisputable that I transformed my body. There's nothing special about me other than the fact that I made the commitment and I brought an unyielding mindset to the process. It takes consistent hard work, tremendous discipline, and tons of effort. But if you're serious about changing your body, you *can* do it. I know you can, because I changed mine.

10

Success: What Is It?

"Action is the foundational key to all success."
—PABLO PICASSO

When I started my podcast, I didn't know where it might lead. I was attracted to the idea of interacting with a range of inspiring and successful people—I was curious and eager to hear what they had to say about their successes. It evolved into a gift that keeps on giving.

In recording every podcast, I am treated to delightful success stories, including the obstacles each guest faced along the way and how they overcame them, what decisions they made and why, how they made good use of the luck they had, and what propelled them to stay focused on their journey.

Their stories run the gamut, from rags-to-riches tales, to how they took shrewd advantage of opportunities that dropped in their path, to how they leveraged their entrepreneurial brilliance. Each story is chock-full of pearls of wisdom and helpful information. For me, the podcast is a treasure trove of inspiration.

Early in the process, on the advice of one of my listeners, I established a signature routine where I'd ask each guest to define success from their personal vantage point. Not surprisingly, the responses have varied as much as their stories. Here are some of my favorites.

Gabe Lubin is the founder and CEO of Cartessa Aesthetics, a New York-based company that manufactures aesthetic medical devices for dermatologists, plastic surgeons, cosmetic physicians, and medical spas.

Gabe grew up in a stable and traditional middle-class family. His dad was a teacher, his mom a social worker. Old school culture grounded family life. His parents earned everything they had through grit and perseverance. As Gabe put it, his parents gave him what he needed, but made it clear that he had to work for what he wanted. I love this because it mirrors how I was raised.

Gabe found tremendous success as a sales executive, but ultimately he decided to take a gamble on himself. He built an eight-figure company from scratch in only a few years. It helped that his wife told him, "I believe in you."

When Gabe founded Cartessa in 2017, he made a market bet. He gambled on Cartessa staying relatively small—to avoid becoming enslaved to shareholder value and the internal politics that often plague larger companies—while distributing best-in-class devices and generating good returns to practitioners. Cartessa is now an international brand.

But when I asked Gabe to define success, he didn't go on about his financial and business achievements and corporate decision-making and risk-taking. He didn't cite chapter and verse about numbers and growth and the balance sheet minutiae that tickles the pockets of investors. He saw personal fulfillment as the pathway to success. To illustrate his point, he shared a story.

He and his wife went to visit his best friend, who was a poor medical student at the time living with his wife and newborn son. At the time, Gabe was a twenty-five-year-old successful salesman living a "baller" lifestyle in downtown Chicago. When he arrived for the visit, he found his friend and young family living in a total dump of an apartment and instantly became concerned about the life circumstances of his good friend and family. What Gabe came away with most from that visit, however, was the sheer joy and love he felt all over the place. It didn't matter that his friend and family were subsisting in a shitty apartment or were financially challenged. They had found a deep and nourishing sweet spot of contentment in family life. It was, for Gabe, an aha -moment about how to value success.

I like to think the seeds of Gabe's epiphany were planted in his humble upbringing from the basic values his family instilled in him. It is often the case that we don't realize the importance of what we learn while young or fully appreciate the moral codes and core values our parents try to impart to us. Often, those lessons tend to simmer beneath the surface until they eventually ease into our lives as we mature and begin to apply what we have been taught.

In Gabe's case, his revelation resonated with how he should run his business: with an abiding appreciation for the people who worked with and surrounded him. He came to describe the work culture at Cartessa as a place where people cared for and strived to respect one another. His leadership style became based on inspiration and inclusion, showing faith and trust in colleagues. As he says on the podcast, "The greatest core asset is human capital."

Gabe's experience ties back to core values. Gabe has uncommon entrepreneurial and business talent and is driven and focused. But he's found success by embracing personal values that transcend business.

Another fascinating guest I had on the podcast was Doug Biro, the founder, director, and producer of Hudson River Films. He produced *Gotti: Godfather & Son*, a four-hour docuseries for A&E. He was also the executive producer of *Getting Naked: A Burlesque Story*, James Lester's award-winning feature documentary about the burlesque scene in New York City. He's worked with famed directors such as David Lynch, David Fincher, and Alex Gibney. He has, by most any measure, enjoyed a successful film career.

He's also had an exhilarating ride in the music world, producing and directing documentaries, promos, and concert films for Norah Jones, Robert Plant, Christina Aguilera, Rufus Wainwright, Kate Hudson, Jerry Lee Lewis, Marion Cotillard, Melody Gardot, Emmy Rossum, Dickey Betts,

Herbie Hancock, Jason Mraz, Tony Bennett, Lady Gaga, and John Fogerty. It's an impressive list.

Doug has enjoyed the kind of big-stage success many of us can only dream about. He knows he's lucky; he knows he's been blessed. Some may even feel that he's led a charmed life. Yet, when I asked him for his definition of success, he didn't focus much on his career at all. He largely equated success with emotional well-being and healthy personal relationships rather than professional achievements. Having been divorced twice, he felt somewhat unsuccessful in the relationship department. He felt successful in the family department, however, through his loving relationship with his college-aged son, which he described with pride and joy, and his strong bonds with his mother and brother.

As an example of what he meant, Doug cited music luminary Herbie Hancock, with whom he has worked extensively. He told me that despite Hancock's extraordinary talent and the many trappings of celebrity status, Hancock has remained a caring and humble human being, which to Doug makes Hancock an ideal model for what success can mean.

Doug's personal transparency connects to emotional intelligence and empathy. No matter what the path to achieving our goal looks like, we'll suffer a substantial shortcoming in our lives—no matter what we've gained—if we don't do right by people, connect with them in ways that respect them for who they are, flaws and all, and see the world through the eyes of the collective. What's the value of achieving a professional or business goal if the process

LET'S GET IT!

that got us there was infected by negativity or littered with unfulfilled relationships?

One of the more interesting discussions about success I had was with Shahzad Qureshi. In addition to real estate sales, Shahzad manages investments in residential new-construction and renovation projects.

Shahzad started out professionally in accounting, a path his dad had taken. When he arrived at the crossroads of long-term decision making in the field, he decided that an accountancy career was not for him. He then pondered law school, figuring that a law degree combined with his accounting background could provide a strong professional foundation that would give him an advantage in the job market. But one day, while immersed in preparing for the LSAT, he realized that a legal career also wasn't the right path for him.

He ultimately teamed up with his father to dabble in real estate, and they enjoyed a modicum of success. Then the itch to captain his own ship became irresistible and he struck out on his own. Now, in his early thirties, he's built a small real estate empire. I was enthralled to hear his story. But his definition of success, like Doug and Gabe's, surprised me.

Shahzad spoke in future terms despite his well-documented financial and business achievements. He said he longed for the day when he could "get out of the twelve-hour-day grind and begin to give back in some capacity." He said he didn't think he would be ready to give back until he could "let off the gas pedal." His definition of success was "when I'm giving more than I'm taking."

It took me a little while to get my head around this definition. Shahzad was saying, in effect, that to succeed, he needed to get to a point where he had both the ability and the time to give back to others on a scale that would allow him to have meaningful and widespread impact. He didn't want to be half-assed; he wanted to be fully engaged in the process. Wow.

This calls up the interactive process discussed earlier. One way or another, we will impact others throughout our lives. How we do so and what we contribute—and to what extent—are for us to decide. Mindless interactions rob us of the opportunity to grow and contribute in positive, enduring ways. Giving back in a thoughtful, focused way, on the other hand, maximizes impact, providing us with a separate and unique sense of purpose apart from everything else we do. Giving back is an important and additional goal to put on our paths.

Shahzad defined success as giving back from a position of strength—he wanted to be in the best position to do so, dialed in and fully engaged. It was on his radar as the ultimate benchmark of success, a place to move toward once he felt that he'd become sufficiently grounded in his own life. What a valuable insight.

This brings me to a classic success story from my podcast guest and close friend Rahsaan Robinson. Rahsaan defined success in a straightforward way, saying it means "accomplishing something you have a true desire to accomplish—whatever that is." Rahsaan is a great example of the hustle and grind mentality.

Rahsaan told me about the day he got lucky when a client treated him to a New York Knicks game in a courtside seat. During pregame warm-ups, Rahsaan became fixated on the trainers working out the athletes and getting them ready for the game. He observed their techniques and the way they communicated with each other. The seriousness with which they approached their craft awed and fascinated him. Sitting there, before tip-off, he said to himself, "I'm going to be out there, on that court. That's what I want to do."

Rahsaan was smart enough to know that he didn't have to reinvent the wheel. He identified others in the field, shadowed them, got tips from them, and learned from them in every way he could. He found receptive mentors and became a sponge. He started working with youth athletes and then moved up to high school athletes and built from there.

Today, Rahsaan is the head strength and conditioning coach for the Long Island Nets, the NBA G League affiliate of the Brooklyn Nets. His path to becoming an elite strength and conditioning coach for a professional sports organization spanned from the early developmental stages of his vision all the way through to the execution of his goal.

Rahsaan's path underscores three important principles discussed earlier: the importance of mentors, tiny wins, and the hustle and grind process. Rashaan knew he had to learn from the many trainers who'd left clues to their successes. He knew he had to move in small steps, slowly climbing the ladder to his goal and putting value in each tiny win. And he knew he had to be vigilant in the process, showing patience and never wavering from his commitment to himself. Rahsaan's story exemplifies everything this book is about.

Celebrity nutritionist Maya Feller also shared a wonderful definition of success. Maya has a fascinating story. Since her childhood, she's had an appreciation for and love of food, which serendipitously evolved to become a major part of her life. In 2005, while she was training for the Boston Marathon, she realized that the science of nutrition fascinated her. She ultimately became a nutrition expert and eventually a media celebrity. As a registered dietitian nutritionist (RDN) in New York, she's dedicated herself to ensuring that her family, community, and clients have access to evidence-based nutrition information and take advantage of high-quality local and organic foods.

In addition to her own practice, Maya has worked as a food and nutrition program manager in an outpatient setting and has partnered with neighborhood community supported agriculture (CSA) programs and food co-ops to bring local and organic food to the community. When working with clients, Maya believes in "meeting the whole person where they are."

Not surprisingly, Maya doesn't view success within the narrow confines of herself. Rather, she defines success within the broader context of the community. For her, success is a litmus test for how she feels about herself, how well her family is doing, and how much impact she's had on the communities she serves. To her, success is a process not an end, a continuous journey that seeks positive, lasting, and infectious changes in the world around her. She seeks to help others discover one change that they can adopt in their lives consistently, which is another way to express the "tiny wins" mindset.

Maya's formulation is a perfect transition to my definition of success, which will come as no surprise: embracing the hustle and grind to reach your goal, whatever it is. If you parse the other definitions, including others from the podcasts not discussed here, it all boils down to a similar mindset: how we engage in the process, what we bring to each small step along the way, looking for those tiny wins, how we impact others during the journey, and how we stay aligned to our commitments and keep pushing the envelope.

The road to success calls on us to tap into our passion, define what success looks like for us in real terms, and challenge ourselves to go after it. The key is what I discussed earlier: looking deeply into our personal mirrors to become critically self-aware and self-honest about who we are and what matters most to us.

What is your definition of success? What do you need to do to achieve it? How committed are you to getting there?

Time is a diminishing asset, and life is too precious to spend doing the bidding of others. The thrill of knowing what burns inside you and giving it full expression is as good as it gets to defining what success is.

The road to the future is wide open. Get on that path, seize its opportunities, celebrate the wins, embrace the failures, and overcome its obstacles. Remember that the accumulation of tiny wins—day after day, week after week, month after month, year after year—are what build to allow to take massive strides toward your goal, provided you trust and love the process and embrace the hustle and grind.

You'll be amazed at what you're capable of accomplishing. Let's get it!

AFTERWORD

The Ten Principles of the Hustle and Grind

1 Life is written by you or for you. You choose.

2 Live by a code of well-considered values and moral principles that reflect who you are and honor everything you do, both professionally and personally.

3 Believe in yourself. Know your power. Trust your instincts.

4 Success leaves clues. Be a sponge. Seek out others you admire and learn from them.

5 Have a plan, avoid shortcuts, trust the process, and execute with patience and passion.

6 In all circumstances, connect with others through kindness, empathy, and a genuine desire to know and affirm them.

7 Find the value in criticism.

8 Failure is the pathway to success.

9 Nutrition is an integral part of what makes you whole.

10 Success isn't a destination, but a process you thoughtfully create for yourself.

ABOUT THE AUTHORS

Adarsh Vijay Mudgil, M.D.

After establishing himself as a highly regarded and sought-after dermatologist in New York City, Dr. Mudgil developed a dynamic social media platform with the aspiration of spreading positivity. In addition to dermatology-related posts, his popular Instagram page includes daily content that explores mindset, motivation, and self-empowerment. He also hosts The Dr. Mudgil Podcast, where he interviews a variety of personalities who share leadership stories and their personal paths to success.

Dr. Mudgil received his bachelor's degree with Phi Beta Kappa honors from Emory University and his medical degree with Alpha Omega Alpha honors from the Renaissance School of Medicine at Stony Brook University. He is a member of the Icahn School of Medicine teaching faculty at Mount Sinai. He has been consistently selected for inclusion on the Super Doctors® list since 2015, which is awarded to about 5 percent of physicians within a respective state or region. He is also listed in the Castle Connolly Top Doctors® guide.

Dr. Mudgil lives in Long Island with his wife, who is a dentist, and his three school-aged children.

Michael J. Coffino

Michael is a published author, memoirist, and ghostwriter, as well as a freelance editor. He started a professional writing career after decades as a business trial attorney, a writing coach to attorneys, and a high school basketball coach. He is an avid hiker, fitness junkie, and martial arts practitioner, and he plays guitar. He was born and raised in the Bronx and lives in Marin County, California.

CPSIA information can be obtained
at www.ICGtesting.com
Printed in the USA
BVHW030228290121
599078BV00010B/222